My Bones Are Red

⚜

A Spiritual Journey
with a Triracial People
in the Americas

My Bones Are Red

A Spiritual Journey
with a Triracial People
in the Americas

Patricia Ann Waak

Mercer University Press
Macon, Georgia USA
2005

ISBN 0-86554-917-6   MUP/P277

My Bones Are Red.
A Spiritual Journey with a Triracial People in the Americas.
Copyright ©2005
Mercer University Press, Macon, Georgia USA
Printed in the United States of America

The paper used in this publication meets the minimum requirements
of American National Standard for Information Sciences—
Permanence of Paper for Printed Library Materials, ANSI Z39.48-1984.

Library of Congress Cataloging-in-Publication Data

Waak, Patricia.
My bones are red : a spiritual journey with a triracial people in the
Americas / Patricia Ann Waak.
   p.   cm.
Includes bibliographical references and index.
ISBN 0-86554-917-6 (pbk. : alk. paper)
   1. Waak, Patricia—Family. 2. Perkins family. 3. Racially mixed
people—United States—Biography. 4. Racially mixed people—
United States—Genealogy. 5. Cherokee Indians—Biography.
6. Cherokee Indians—Genealogy. 7. Pioneers—Louisiana—Biography. 8. Pioneers—Texas—Biography. 9. Louisiana—Biography.
10. Texas—Biography.
   I. Title.
E184.A1W114 2005
929'.2'08905970073—dc22

                                                    2004014604

Contents

* * *

For Anise Dominique Savoy Baldi.
In memory of
Anne Nell Smith Waak,
Dooley Wirt Smith,
and Martha Mary Perkins Smith.

Preface and Acknowledgments

The journey to find my ancestry and its meaning for my own life began almost a decade before I began filling shelves and file drawers with papers and books that still accumulate. However, it was during my three years of study for a Doctor of Ministry degree that I had "permission" to draw together some of this material. So I responded with great appreciation to Dr. Dorsey Blake's suggestion that I do my dissertation project on the story of my triracial ancestors. Thanks to Dr. Cristina Gonzalez and Dr. H. L. Goodall, Jr., I discovered the autoethnobiographical approach. The dissertation project unfolded into a manuscript composed of stories about the history of a people's quest for recognition and respect.

I thank all my recovered "cousins" who shared their research and information. In particular, Shirley Conrad made frequent trips to the genealogical records at the Houston, Texas, library to obtain copies of censuses and tax records. Randy Willis shared his files with us via e-mail. Sandra Loridans tirelessly provided documentation and was instrumental in helping me to recover Columbus Perkins and make the connections with other cousins. Erbon Wise shared his research and allowed me to go through his files, as did Hazel Stanley. More recently, William Duty and Brian Rick gave access to their files.

Correspondence with the Gowens Foundation opened numerous doors in tracking down clues on the origins of the Perkins family. I am especially thankful to Arlee Gowen. Cousin Lee Murrah provided his accounts from the data he has collected and came to visit me in Colorado to share stories and questions.

I am deeply grateful for the assistance of Paul Heinegg, especially before I was able to get a copy of his wonderful book. By electronic mail, he sent portions that were pertinent and provided moral support as we took on the tough job of finding all extant records. Dr. Virginia DeMarce also gave of her time and her perspective. I am grateful for her guidance and advice. Her scientific articles have been heavily criticized by some, but I have no doubt about her conclusions. To Brent Kennedy I give my thanks for his encouragement and enthusiasm when it came time to publish.

The assistance of Dr. Jim Teer and Pat McGuill in helping us find the Laurence Wood Cemetery and get access to it was most appreciated. We are grateful to Shannon Wood for giving us access and her husband, Chris Bush, for guiding us to the site.

It is impossible to express appreciation to all the people who treated my husband, Kenneth Strom, and me with respect and dignity in the Accomack County Courthouse, the Bladen County Courthouse, the Knox County Library, the U.S. National Archives, the Sam Houston Regional Library, and the Texas State Archives. We are especially grateful to Keith Fontenot, archivist for the St. Landry Parish Clerk of Courts in Opelousas, Louisiana. He found rare documents and went out of his way to make sure we carried away the best copies. And Sally Polhemus provided reproductions of the famous Tennessee case involving Jacob Perkins and John White.

The most long-suffering of all these public servants must be the staff of the Goliad County Courthouse. We return again and again to Goliad and find new items for our research each time. We are always treated cordially.

My family has been an inspiration. My dad, Boxly Waak, has served as an example by persistently tracing his side of the family and meticulously documenting each member. His files are some of the most complete I have ever seen. My sister, Linda Waak Beasley, has reminded me of the spiritual blessings we have in this family. My brothers, Roger and Don Waak, have shown great interest and provided support and have been free to share their memories of Granddaddy Smith. Roger, and his son Graham, also spent time in the Texas State Archives searching for and copying pages from old microfilm. Our children—Cinira Baldi, Rachel Baldi Carter, Melissa Beasley, Jon David Beasley, Erika Waak Marcoux, Graham Waak, Betsy Waak, and William "Trey" Waak—are the beautiful manifestations of this family's soul. My parents' surviving great-grandchildren, Anise Baldi, Brandon Charles Waak, and Jordan Waak are the recipients of the struggles and joys of their ancestors. And the late little Isaiah Barrington Carter reminds us of all the little male children who came as messengers and left us the blessings of their short lives.

The process has been mine as I recover the past of my family, but my dear husband, Kenneth Strom, makes this journey with me. His methodical and careful eye found documents that I would have missed. His interest in the land transfers helped trace the lives of individuals. He deserves much of the credit for helping to identify and connect the Red Bones with my

Granddaddy Smith. He has embraced this family as his own. I am so grateful for his wisdom, intellect, and faith.

I must thank my mother, Anne Nell Smith Waak, for her encouragement and assistance in tracing stories and finding documentation for various family myths and legends. She expressed such joy as each new discovery was made and was with us when we found the cemetery where her great-grandfather is buried. We did not find her grandmother Martha's grave as she longed to, but the journey will go on. Mother did not live to see this particular project completed, but her spirit was with me as I wrote each chapter. I will always miss her, but her grace, hope, and joyous prodding have made me the person I am.

It has been my joy to work with Lise Rousseau over a number of years in Audubon. She has brought many of my communication ideas to life through her technical skills. Thanks to her, the photos and charts that give face and name to the people in the pages are here to clarify.

As you read through the pages, remember that a "myth" is just an old story. We are left with pieces of fabric, some shiny and some faded. Our hearts must be open if we are to see the whole. No matter how much documentation we find, it only tells us as much as it can. It is as incomplete as the old story itself when viewed out of context. This book is one attempt at putting all the pieces together while being faithful to old stories and new dreams.

Erie, Colorado*Patricia Waak Strom*

A Waak Photo Album

1. *Henry Christian Waak*
and Hulda Fredericka Timme.

2. August Timme and Augusta Mahnke.

3. My father, Boxly William Waak, in 1942.

4. My mother, Anne Nell Waak, at seventeen.

5. *My maternal grandmother,*
Annie Elizabeth Jane Mayes, 1902.

6. L. Bridge and Susie Elizabeth Mayes,
my mother's great-grandparents.

7. *Nathan Gann and Aletha Jane Aldredge,*
my mother's great-great-grandparents.

8. My *mother's great-grandparents,*
Nathan Aldredge and Mary Elizabeth Mayes Gann,
and children.

9. *Dooley Wirt Smith, my maternal grandfather.*

10. My mother's parents, Granddaddy and Grandma Smith.

*11. Boxly Waak and Nell Waak
with their first child, Patricia Ann Waak.*

12. Dooley Smith with grandchildren.
Top row: Linda and Patricia Waak, Frank and Mary Woolf.
Bottom row: Jerry Woolf, Bubba Berry,
Donald and Roger Waak.

13. *Sarco Cemetery, Goliad, Texas.*

14. Columbus Perkins and his wife Willie.

15. Columbus Perkins at a later date.

*16. Jordan Perkins,
my great-grandmother's brother.*

17. Laurence Wood Cemetery, outside Goliad, Texas.

18. Grave of Keziah Perkins Bundick,
Laurence Wood Cemetery, Goliad, Texas.

19. Grave of Jesse Perkins,
Laurence Wood Cemetery, Goliad, Texas.

20. Senegal and Gambia countryside.

21. Goliad prairie near Sarco Creek, Texas.

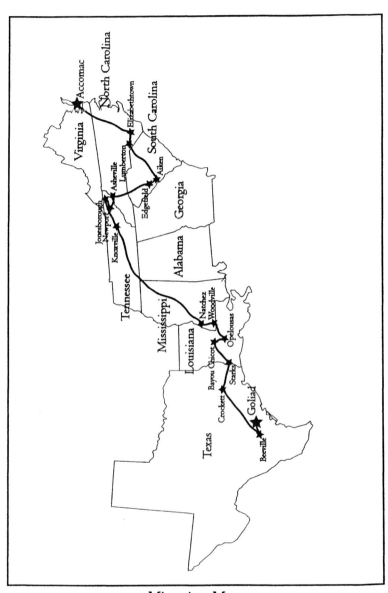

Migration Map

Chapter 1

My Bones Are Red

We are descendants of Red Bones.[1] I proudly state that after centuries of assimilation and hidden histories shrouded in mystery. The true story of the Red Bones and their origins is practically untraceable. But this is *my* story, *my* mystery, uncovered from countless written records and oral traditions.

The search for the story of these mixed-race people is built out of a yearning to know who I am and who they were. The search is also about retrieving the body of the family and recovering a history that has been blurred at best and erased at worst. The term *recover* is used, instead of discover, because this journey is one of laying claim to the truth of a people and their gifts to their descendants.

If in the "white" world you are asked to introduce yourself, your response will be in terms of your name, occupation, or a major accomplishment. In the American Indian world, the response is a recitation of lineage. Therefore, "My name is Pat and I am a psychologist and theologian"

---

[1]The origin of the term "Red Bones" and its meaning is uncertain. See esp. my note in "The Path of Darkness," prelude to chap. 6, below. Here we may note that some modern dictionaries have dropped the term "Red Bone(s)" altogether, and include *only* the totally unrelated "redbone" (one word), the latest *Webster's Collegiate's* (2003) definition of which is typical: "any of a breed of agile speedy coonhounds of U.S. origin having a usu. solid dark red coat." The earlier definition of "red bone" (two words) in *Webster's Third New International Dictionary* (1981) may still be cited as a generally accepted definition: "red bone *n. usu cap R & B* 1 : one of a group of people of mixed white, Indian, and Negro ancestry esp. in Louisiana— often used disparagingly. 2. CROATAN." (We may note that the supposed synonym [?] "Croatan"—to be distinguished of course from "Croatian"—also seems to have disappeared from current dictionaries.) Finally, while the term occurs in the literature as both one word (Redbones) and two (Red Bones), it seems best to retain the lowercase one-word "redbone" for the coonhound and the capitalized two-word "Red Bones" for the persons.

My bones are red.

Interlaced with the trails my ancestors followed.
Merging with other travelers,
losing their identity while sharing their strength.

My bones are red.
Exotic peoples filled with adventure, daring and rage,
Fighting for some semblance of place and recognition.

My bones are red.
It is the structure of who I am.

becomes "My name is Pat and I am the daughter of Boxly and Nell Waak, the granddaughter of Henry and Hulda Waak, the granddaughter of Dooley and Annie Smith, etc."

Family history has become important to millions of Americans. For us— in my case, for the Waaks, Timmes, Smiths, and Perkins—family history provides a texture to our lives. My own life has been graced with opportunity for expression on some of the most important issues of our time. However, there is a deep longing to know the people who gave me the gift of life. So in the midst of a world filled with motherhood, work, and study, I always made some space to look for my great-grandmother, Martha Mary Perkins Smith.

Martha Mary Perkins Smith was Dooley Smith's mother. She died when Granddaddy Smith was nine years old. She was the root of an old story that Granddaddy was a Cherokee Indian. I would discover that many people in the Southern United States, especially, claim Cherokee Indian heritage. Given my grandfather's practices of interpreting dreams and other tales of healing with his hands, the Indian connection seemed credible. But Granddaddy remembered little about his mother, so I was intent on finding out who she was, what tribe she came from and which part of the country was her "homeland."

That search intensified as I, like so many others interested in their ancestry, discovered the potential of the Internet to connect otherwise separated and unknown people. On the night of my birthday, February 1, 1995, I received an electronic message from George Goins, which opened the door to the stories told in these pages. He told me that his people came from Louisiana and were related to the Perkins family by marriage. George also gave me a list of "cousins" to contact. That message took me across the country into dusty archives and unexplored cemeteries in Virginia, South Carolina, Tennessee, Louisiana, and Texas. Sometimes we found nothing. Other times we recovered whole stories left amidst carefully handwritten records from another century.

The only identified root of this family may have been a woman named Esther Perkins. In 1730 a wealthy landowner paid a fine on her behalf. The fine was levied because she gave birth to an illegitimate child. Was she white? Those people recorded in the early 1800s who bore her name were listed as "Free Negroes."[2]

---

[2]U.S. Bureau of the Census, Accomack Parish & St. George's Parish Household

Historical accounts indicate that free blacks owned land in Virginia and Maryland as far back as the late 1600s.[3] Were the names in the old censuses their original names? Were they free Africans? Had they ever been slaves or indentured servants? Did they take the names of their owners? The Perkins name is one of those found among these questions. While the only people named Perkins in Accomack County, Virginia were listed as mulatto, there is a record of a "white" Isaac Perkins living in Maryland in early colonial records.[4]

Two children named Perkins were "bound out" to a man named Gibson. Did this make them indentured servants? If you were mulatto, did you become indentured rather than a slave? Was there any difference? Was this a free white woman who had children with a black man? The children were orphans. Was this the practice with mulatto children?

And then there is the story of the Carolinas, and the rice farmers from Barbados who worked the fields. Many of the people of the Caribbean Islands came from the western coast of Africa. Were these my people? Was I drawn to Brazil as a young woman because I come from the same triracial stock as northeastern Brazil coastal people? Do I understand better the washing out and in of genetics because of that experience?

A thousand questions lie among the scattered pages of dusty books and leaves on trails across America. A thousand lies hide the people who struggled to make a place for themselves in a world that was "colorless." And here I am, generations later, trying to reclaim with pride what they may have hidden for reasons of acceptance and survival. Given the number of books about mixed-race people today, perhaps the world has changed. However, I still see strange stares directed at interracial couples.

Most of our ancestry contributes in some way to customs carried over in families. Genetics has made it important to know who our forebears were and the most common types of diseases or causes of death they encountered. But as a theologian I believe we have a spiritual heritage as well. By that I do not necessarily mean a religious tradition, although I believe the Red Bones carried that as well. Spiritual tradition affects the way we look at the world and interact with it. It may complement religious practice, but it is

---

Enumeration, Accomack, Virginia, 1800.

[3]Paul Heinegg, *Free African Americans of North Carolina and Virginia* (Baltimore: Clearfield, 1997) 1-2.

[4]Sandra M. Loridans, personal correspondence, 1997.

much more fundamental in how we see our place in the universe and how we see family.

My spirituality has always been connected to Creation, which is not in opposition with what we are taught in Christian theology. Wandering through the woods, listening to birds, following insects always helped me center myself. I studied other religions over the years and developed my own eclectic formulation of worship and ritual. However, my work with indigenous groups in other countries and Native Americans in the United States drew me most deeply into those spiritual practices.

The theology of Creation Spirituality has helped me to structure the meaning we give to the story of our past. Creation Spirituality grew out of the Christian mystics of the Middles Ages. In its purest form Creation Spirituality defines four paths: Via Positiva, Via Negativa, Via Creativa, and Via Transformativa.[5] I have given these paths new names in order to frame the stories of my ancestors. The first path is a path of life-affirming blessing, so I call it the Path of Blessing. We see Creation as that blessing and we move away from the theology that we are all born in original sin and must be redeemed. Original blessing is what we celebrate; the fact that we have the gift of life is reason to rejoice.

The second path contains the principle of embracing the dark. We so often talk of seeking the light or enlightenment. In Creation Spirituality, theologian Matthew Fox describes this as emptying or letting go and letting be. However, it is more than looking at darkness in a different way; it is actually befriending the darkness and what it brings to us. Rather than running away from the problems of the world, we must face them and allow the pain to be pain.[6] So we embrace the second path as the Path of Darkness. It is a way to learn meaning in our lives and that of our families.

To be in the center of issues that focus so basically on life has to be part of befriending creation. To devote one's life to the world demands the bearing of enormous pain. The gift is to find a way to create and transform which ultimately leads to the next two paths. Therefore, the third path unites the blessing of life with the possibility of creativity. Fox describes it thus: "letting both pleasure and pain happen, both light and darkness, we allow the very power of birth."[7]

---

[5]Matthew Fox, *Original Blessing* (Santa Fe NM: Bear, 1983) 127.

[6]Fox, *Original Blessing*, 142.

[7]Fox, *Original Blessing*, 175.

In these stories from the past we return to our roots to understand the community of my own family. The Path of Creativity then becomes the third path. It is filled with song, dance, and adventure. It may begin as simply as the belief that we can heal ourselves and Earth by telling our stories.

The moment we let go of all the things we believe are important is the moment we give birth to something new. At least that is my personal epiphany. It is the Path of Creativity. When we let go of the place where we are, we can begin to create a new place, a new path, and a new journey. The leap of faith comes with being able to push out of the old structures. The future is a dance, no less mysterious then the past or present. But reimaging the world and our space in it must be one of the most creative ventures of all.

Matthew Fox talks of the biblical teaching on creativity. He says "that every person is endowed with the divine power of birthing."[8] He stresses here the emphasis on speaking through our own creative possibilities. It may be singing, painting, writing, or some other art form. For some, it is expressing oneself in a new way. How amazing that we never hear it explained that way. Human creativity flows out of Creation and we are called to be what we have the capacity to be.

In the fourth path, the Path of Transformation, we are called to "make" justice in the world. In writing some years ago about the principles of justice, I found myself inspired to separate out three types of justice. Social justice is applied to the condition of humans in the world, including issues of poverty and environmental health. Ecojustice encompasses the rights of existence and health for other life on this planet that is not considered human. Intergenerational justice is based on what we bequeath to that life to come, human and other.

The form of justice one takes depends on each individual. It also relies on the experience of the particular generation. The Red Bones were looking for social justice. It was the most immediate challenge before them. Today their descendants may be immersed in social-justice issues, but ecojustice has become paramount for many of us as we watch the sacred creation of our home being destroyed. What we share is the desire for intergenerational justice that comes out of strong tribal family ties.

---

[8]Fox, *Original Blessing*, 184.

Hopefully we carry the wisdom of those in our past. For us, their descendants, the story is still to be written. How we each claim that story will be different, but we will be embraced by all the pain and joy from the tales told in dusty pages and vague memories.

For me in establishing this new place in the accounts of my ancestors, this center of power and revelation, it is important to understand my roots, or as I prefer, my gifts. Luisah Teish states it as the African belief that "those who go before us make us what we are."[9]

So I have chosen to apply the four paths of Creation Spirituality to the joyful yet troubled lives of my ancestors. For what they faced, regardless of their origins, was discrimination based on color, something my siblings, my cousins and I have not had to contend with. The reason we did not have to endure racism based on the color of our skin is that my ancestors transformed themselves into the mainstream of society, whether that was their intent or not.

While present-day family members enjoy the fruits of our ancestors hard work and heritage, we are rediscovering their stories. This same desire has been strong in my parents and their children. Each struggle of every generation has been for the American ideal that you can accomplish anything by working at it.

I have characterized my upbringing as an attempt to straddle some invisible line between the rational and the intuitive. My father's need for structure and the German culture of his upbringing is steeped in the rational. My mother's mystical personality and her part-Native American heritage seem to connect with the intuitive. It is my mother's family stories that begin to profile the forgotten past of so many people in the Southern United States.

My maternal grandfather's people were triracial, at least from what we know. These triracial people are not only a great mystery in my family; they represent a little-documented aspect of American history. Often, instead of rejoicing in their strength and courage, different family groups argue about the nature of their origins. The most vociferous speakers are those descendants who seem to fear the discovery of "black" African heritage. "Black" African is emphasized because some of these descendants accept "North" African Moors yet reject the possibility of the ancestors originating from the people of Senegal, Gambia or Angola.

---

[9]Luisah Teish, *Jambalaya* (San Francisco: Harper, 1985) 68.

Although racism and bigotry may be at the heart of this debate, it also relates to fear. The first concern is the loss of the longed for respectability which generations have striven for during the assimilation process. Associations with what might be considered an underclass are difficult because whether we admit it or not, the world has various strata of people rated by some according to color of skin, wealth, or gender, as well as other categories. For the triracial families, race was a hindrance, and they shed layers as they migrated west.

The second, not-unrelated fear or anxiety is the deepseated angst over false accusation. It lives buried in so many of the descendants, swallowed and physically manifested in stomach disorders. These triracial families lived for generations on the edge of other societies. Many of them were described as outlaws. Others feared that anything that went wrong would be blamed on them. For this reason, the Red Bone families stayed together, moving as one to avoid problems.[10]

The survival of each individual and family group has been a story of spiritual connection to Earth and other creatures. The tradition of membership in the Baptist denomination of Christianity has provided an ongoing community for a people who have tribal connections, or at least did so for over a century. However, there is strong evidence of African and Native American spiritual principles in values and fundamental beliefs. I have attempted to identify those which seem most pertinent to this family.

The great African American mystic, Dr. Howard Thurman, once spoke of "a long quest into my own past as the deep resource for finding my way into wholeness in the present."[11] I will only add that the quest goes on for all of our lives as we reclaim the gifts and come to know our own family history.

---

[10]Gary B. Mills, "Tracing Free People of Color in the Antebellum South: Methods, Sources, and Perspectives," *National Genealogical Society Quarterly* 78 (December 1990): 266.

[11]Sudershan Kapur, *Raising Up a Prophet: The African-American Encounter with Gandhi* (Boston: Beacon Press, 1992) 82.

The Path of Blessing

The four paths of Creation Spirituality provide an inspiration and structure for the organization of these stories. The first is the Path of Blessing and is described as "a path of affirmation, thanksgiving, ecstasy."[1] Or better, Fox calls it "falling in love with existence."[2] I love this concept for I believe the Perkins family whose story I am unraveling must have been a constant source of joy and revelry. The descendants are filled with music and celebration. Their "tribe" expresses this hopefulness in their existence despite illness, death, and despair. They must have needed this optimistic view of the world to survive the discrimination and resulting perils of migration.

Chapters 2, 3, 4, and 5, are a celebration of the Path of Blessing for a people who found ways to survive and flourish. These chapters trace this people's journey into Louisiana at the beginning of the nineteenth century. To celebrate their joys and pains I have begun each chapter with a poem of remembrance.

Their story is no less phenomenal today than it was hundreds of years ago. It is the great adventure of individual dreams, aspirations and ambition. Even though we are the current generations, the blood of our ancestors still pushes us on to monumental dreaming and achievement.

---

[1]Fox, *Original Blessing*, 33.
[2]Fox, *Original Blessing*, 39.

There is a welling in the depths of my soul
Which sings of heart and courage and love.
There is a longing within some darkened place
That calls me home to grace and comfort.
These wellings and longings are always there
Inherited and granted from those who came before?
They define my joy.
They bring me bliss.
They frame my tears.
They give me substance.
Who are these people who call from within my blood
And bones
And skin?
My skin is pink, but I am called white.
My bones are white, but I know they are red.
My blood is dark blue, but it is the black of beginning.
They came from Africa and Europe and America
And bound our hopes and dreams as one.
We celebrate our differences yet are called to be unnamed.
And somewhere in our souls we know that we are the
Embodiment of the aspirations of all these peoples.
It is our gift and our legacy.

Chapter 2

The Song of the Ancestors

In 1854, a man named Heinrich Waak arrived in the port of New Orleans. Because of him, I am "white." He had traveled from Rovershagen, Germany, aboard a ship bound for the Americas. The family story is that he had an argument with his brother and left to find his fortune. As we now know from an accumulation of histories, Heinrich was probably not the firstborn and would not inherit his father's land. So he had to emigrate in order to have land of his own. We know he traveled with his wife and three children. One of the children died en route.

There is not much known about the family Heinrich left behind. According to his later accounts, he was a citizen of Mecklenburg. The name had originally been spelled Waack, which means "he who lives in the sign of the wolf."[1] Because of the double "a" in the name, it is possible that this family descended from the Friesian people who lived on the upper coast of the Netherlands and were brought to Mecklenburg by Henry the Lion (1129–1195) in the Middle Ages. Their livelihood was then farming and that would be their chief industry for centuries to come.

Heinrich Waak was one of a number of German families who migrated to Texas in the mid-1800s. He disembarked at New Orleans, took another boat to Galveston, then loaded his family in a cart and traveled to an area around Cat Springs, Texas, that became part of a band of German-speaking communities. By 1870, fifteen percent of the German-born farmers in Austin County, Texas, where Cat Springs was located, were from Mecklenburg, the highest percentage in the county.[2]

---

[1]Roger Waak, personal communication, 1994. My brother studied German as an undergraduate, and Russian while doing his graduate work in European history. In general, the family seems to have a facility for languages. My linguistic proficiency includes Portuguese and Spanish. Great-grandfather Charles Smith was said to speak seven languages.

[2]Terry G. Jordan, *German Seed in Texas Soil* (Austin: University of Texas Press,

One of Heinrich's grandsons was Henry Christian Waak. Henry was a farmer like his father and grandfather. Though many of the farmers began with the planting and harvesting of wheat and rye, they turned to crops primarily of corn and cotton.[3] In addition, the Waak family produced hay for sale and sweet potatoes for their own consumption. My father recalls a plot of 180 acres of river bottom that his father, Henry, devoted to raising cotton.[4]

Henry borrowed heavily from his father in order to have seed, machinery and other tools for working the land. Unfortunately, he also had a corn-liquor still. Bottles of corn liquor were hidden under the loose corn in the bin. They were for his consumption. Alcoholism would contribute heavily to his early demise.

Henry married Hulda Fredericka Timme, a daughter of August Timme and Augusta Mahnke (photo 1). August had also traveled from Germany to farm in Texas, and Augusta was a first generation German immigrant herself (photo 2). Their daughter, Hulda, was a tiny, spirited woman, who would become a nurse in later years. Her husband died when my father was six years old. He left Hulda deeply in debt, and her father-in-law took the land and equipment to pay off a bank note. He tried to take her children as well, but she moved onto her parents' land. There, she planted and chopped cotton which her only son, Boxly, took to market to sell.

My father, Boxly Waak, grew up living next to his great-uncle, Ben Timme, and his grandparents. German was the common language in the household. Growing up from six years of age into adolescence was difficult for the only boy. He was constantly "fathered" by every man in the family. As a result, my father lied about his age and joined the army at seventeen. A tall and handsome young man, he quickly became recognized for his intelligence and energy. Without a high school diploma, he was still selected for Officers Candidate School (photo 3).

At eighteen, he went to visit George and Lois Thomason with an Army buddy. Sitting in the corner of the room was a ten-year-old girl named Annie Nell Smith, Lois's little sister. Bright, shy, and precocious would probably be appropriate adjectives for my mother at that age. They would not meet again until she was fifteen. And in this second meeting they would

---

1994) 64.

[3]Jordan, *German Seed in Texas Soil*, 94.

[4]Boxly Waak, personal Communication. 2000.

fall in love. Mother later said she was anxious to get away from home so she was ready to marry Daddy (photo 4). There was always this synergy that completed the two. He brought stability into her life, and she brought an intuitive gentleness into his.

My maternal grandmother was Annie Elizabeth Jane Mayes (photo 5). Her parents were John Mayes of Kentucky and Mary Emma Gann. John's parents were L. Bridge Mayes and Susie Elizabeth Mayes (photo 6). We have less information about the Mayes side of the family. They probably came to Texas from Kentucky in the 1800s when most of the migration was taking place because they were there in 1849.

On the Gann side, Ignatious Nathan Gann was born in 1759 in Virginia.[5] He moved to Tennessee early on, where he owned vast acres of land near the Nolichucky River. His grandson, Nathan Wilson Gann, received a Texas land grant in 1841.[6] In order to obtain this land he had to prove that he had arrived in Texas on or before March 1, 1836. That would have made Nathan Wilson Gann one of the early American settlers of Texas. Nathan married Aletha Jane Aldredge, who had arrived from Mississippi with her family in 1833 (photo 7).

The second of their ten children, Nathan Aldredge Gann was Mary Emma's father (photo 8) and my grandmother's grandfather. Although the general story on this side of the family is that the Ganns were Scotch-Irish and possibly French, the name Gann is listed as both a triracial isolate,[7] and as one of the mixed race people called Melungeons.[8] Although not the centerpiece of my research, the Gann origins were significant in light of what we learned about the heritage of my mother's father.

My mother's father was named Dooley Wirt Smith (photo 9). His father, Charles Smith, had been born in Virginia and came to Texas with Dooley's grandfather, Alexander, between 1840 and 1950. Charles had been

---

[5]William R. Gann and Gary R. Toms, *The Ignatious Nathan Gann Family: Three Generations of Pioneers* (Raytown MO: Gann and Toms, 1998) 1.

[6]Gann and Toms, *The Ignatious Nathan Gann Family*, 246.

[7]Angela Y. Walton-Raji, *Black Indian Genealogy Research: African American Ancestors among the Five Civilized Tribes* (Bowie MD: Heritage Books, 1993) 139.

[8]N. Brent Kennedy with Robyn Vaughan Kennedy, *The Melungeons: The Resurrection of a Proud People* (Macon GA: Mercer University Press 1994) 148. "Triracial isolate" is a term used for a group of people with combined European, African, and Native American heritage. They tended to live separately from others in their community and intermarry among like families.

a stagecoach driver in the mid-1800s and by 1870 was teaching school in Goliad, Texas. His mother, Louise Guthridge, probably died in Virginia because his father would later marry Amelia Jane Carter and raise a second family in Texas,

The focus of this story, however, is on Dooley and his maternal ancestors. We were always told that Granddaddy was a Cherokee Indian. Even today, two of my mother's surviving brothers refer to Grandpa Smith as a Cherokee Indian. Up until ten years before this writing, the Smith family history was confused and filled with conflicting stories but seemed to be pretty straightforward about the Indian ancestry.

By 1989, I had composed an autobiography for a psychology class. It was the first attempt at setting out the details of who I was and the nature of what we carried from our ancestors. My biography began like this. "I was born of pioneers and pacifists. They loved the land and believed that their time was best spent tending crops than fighting someone else's battles." Captain Charles W. Smith was accused of abandoning the Civil War. He probably had gone home to tend his crops. August Timme definitely had fled the compulsory conscription of Germany. He was supposed to be home on leave when he got on a boat to the United States.[9]

My great-grandfather, Charles Smith, and his father, Alexander, were farmers and soldiers. Alexander is referred to as "General" on the death certificate of one of his daughters.[10] We have never determined the source of his officer's rank since the name Smith is quite common and many soldiers were listed under their first initial. Could it have been an honorary title of respect?

The Smith families probably came from Scotland or Ireland. They appear to be landholders in Texas. That was not uncommon, since the wresting of Texas from Spain included the granting of land to everyone who arrived. The Republic of Texas continued that practice.

In addition to being a teacher, Charles Smith was a county surveyor and justice of the peace.[11] There are many documents of land transactions that he implemented and notes from a survey of bounty lands filed with the

---

[9]Boxly Waak, personal Communication.

[10]Death Certificate for Annie Mary Cowan, 13698, 1933. Texas State Department of Health: Bureau of Vital Statistics.

[11]Bond hearing for Chas. W. Smith as County Surveyor in Goliad County, Commissioners Court Special Session, 28 March 1899.

Goliad County Courthouse.[12] Charles appeared to be a well-educated man, for—as mentioned earlier—according to family tradition he spoke seven languages.

It was Charles's wife, Martha Mary Perkins, who claimed to be a Cherokee Indian. In the 1880 Census, her parents were listed as being born in the Old Indian Nation in Rome, Georgia.[13] This census record would serve as a focal point for debate and research. In 1989, there was speculation that Martha and her family came to Texas during the forced march of the Cherokee Nation. That theory proved to be guesswork of one cousin and not correct as far as we can ascertain.

Martha and Charles together produced eight children, of which there were two sets of twins (chart 1). One of their sons was my grandfather, Dooley Wirt Smith. He would do as much for keeping the family mystery alive as anyone. Granddaddy Dooley married Annie Elizabeth Jane Mayes in Mountain City, Texas on January 20, 1907. Grandma's family was not happy with this match. They believed she had married beneath herself. But although my grandparents did not always agree on everything, they were married for more than fifty years (photo 10).

Grandma Smith was a strong, often severe, woman of courage and perseverance. I do not remember them going to church, but she had a spiritual air about her. Mother told me that Grandma was a lifelong member of the Buda Methodist Church. Although Granddaddy called himself a Baptist, he did not attend formal services. According to my mother and her younger brother, Granddaddy read the Bible daily and believed that the past, present, and future could be found in its pages.

Between them my grandparents produced ten living children (chart 2). The youngest daughter, and next-to-youngest child, was my mother, Anne Nell. Nell, as she was called, was an extremely intelligent and well-read woman. Yet she left school at the age of fifteen and married my father, eight years her senior. She said that after the death of one of her older sisters, her parents brought in a granddaughter near her same age. Conflicts between her and her niece caused my mother to look for a means of escape.

Mother's early life was spent around military bases. Dad's formal education almost entirely was obtained through his military service. After Officer's Candidate School he rose to the rank of captain. He spent the rest

---

[12]Boundary Survey. Goliad County Courthouse, Goliad TX, 1876).
[13]U.S. Bureau of the Census, Inhabitants of Callahan County Texas, 1800, 356.

of his working life in the military reserves and in the government, rising through the ranks on the merits of his intelligence and hard work. My parents traveled with me, their firstborn, to different locations in the United States (photo 11). In 1950, we settled in Conroe, Texas as a family of six; three siblings had been added (chart 3). Daddy worked for the U.S. Post Office until he retired. Upon his retirement, Daddy went back to growing things on a small piece of land, returning to his first love.

Setting out to tell the story of a family is a formidable task. Which events are most important and how you present those selected in a way that paints a distinct picture of a person's trials and accomplishments is not easy. The story I will try to tell is even more challenging because it is my life and more. The story is one of a people. I do not have old pictures of them like my other ancestors. Complicating things more was a mystery that lay hidden for at least two or three generations. Where I discovered it was in some faint, fine memories of my grandfather.

My grandfather, Dooley Wirt Smith, was already sixty-six years old when I was born. My mother was born when Dooley was forty-seven years old. Mother had not reached her seventeenth birthday when I was born. My memories of him seem the richest when I was around five years of age.

Grandfathers are magic to little girls. I only had one. While my great-uncle Ben Timme served as godfather to me, and I loved him dearly, it was not quite the same as being my grandfather. Both of these men seemed exotic.

Uncle Ben smelled of baby chicks and cows. He was a lifelong bachelor farmer. As a first generation German immigrant, his speech still carried the thick accent of his parents' homeland. I always guessed that he only spoke English to those of us who did not speak German.

But it was Granddaddy Smith who served the role of confidante, teacher, and magician. He smelled of pipe tobacco and old clothes. It was a rich, full smell that attracted me to the smell of pipe tobacco for the rest of my life. He had bad knees from years of breaking horses, but it never prevented him from finding a place for a small girl to perch. He also had those favorite expressions that captured a child's fancy. Anything that surprised him was responded to by, "Well I'll be jump up and down!" It was not just the words. It was the inflection and facial expressions. His tone and style made it one of the funniest of his commentaries, and it is one of the most vivid memories of my sister today.

I remember the years when Granddaddy would say, "Let's go see your cousins." He would pile us into his car and take us to the Breckenridge Park

Zoo's Monkey Island in San Antonio. So it was Grandpa Smith who introduced us to the theory of evolution long before the big discussions in schools and churches. It was at this same zoo where I rode my first elephant at the age of six. If he could only have seen me forty years later riding an elephant through the Royal Chitwan Jungle of Nepal.

Of course what he was really teaching us was about our connection to nature. Long summer evenings sitting in his yard watching the bats fly were part of the celebration of Creation. Today, we cannot see bats flying overhead without listening for the tinkling of the ice cream truck. They are forever associated with the pleasure of a warm twilight filled with the love of that old man.

Of all the interesting things about my granddaddy, two stood out the most. His books probably went unnoticed by many in the family, but they were extraordinary to me. I was ever and am always the ultimate bookworm. Memories magnify size, but in his tiny room there seemed to be hundreds of books on astrology and dream interpretation. I was mesmerized as a young girl. Dreams fascinated me. Astrology was a mystery although I knew that many people read horoscopes. My mother remembers the astrology part. She said that most people found it amusing or silly when Granddaddy offered to read their horoscopes.

The second interesting bit about Granddaddy was that he was "part" Indian. The family story was that Charles Smith had married a woman who was a Cherokee. Granddaddy told me that he was half-Indian. However, my mother said that her grandmother was one-quarter Cherokee. Like so many Americans who carry the family stories of being part Indian, Mother claimed that Martha Perkins Smith's mother was the granddaughter of an Indian Chief. The verification of this was pointed to in the census rolls where the writer entered "Old Indian Nation."[14]

This heritage was related through oral history and never verified. My grandfather died on November 16, 1958. As far as I can tell, no one attempted to get more information from him. My uncles said that he did not talk much about his family. Dooley's mother died when he was nine years old. His father, Charles, married Zilpha Holbrook in 1893.

Dooley did not like his stepmother so he ran away from home at the age of thirteen with his younger brothers and sister. According to Granddaddy, he loaded up his smaller brothers and sister onto a buckboard wagon

---

[14]Ibid.

and drove them to his older married sister's house. Zilpha Holbrook Smith called the sheriff who went off to get the children back and "arrest" Granddaddy. The sheriff discovered them at Aunt Lucretia's house, who was married to one of Zilpha Holbrook Smith's sons. The children were allowed to stay at Aunt Lucretia's, and Granddaddy was not arrested.

When I asked my grandparents about my bloodline from Mother's side of the family, they would respond Scotch, Irish, French, and Cherokee Indian. Somehow I assumed that Grandma Smith was the Scotch and Irish side and Granddaddy was the French and Cherokee Indian. His complexion was darker than Grandma's. However, when I got to a certain point in my own discovery, it became clearer that the "Cherokee Indian" heritage was much more complicated.

It would take years to unravel the matted threads of the past. In the 1950s Granddaddy went back to Goliad to claim some inheritance from the sale of cattle.[15] One of my uncles accompanied him but was not able to remember whom they went to see or any of the details. There are stories of a cousin who was either in the state legislature of Texas or working in the state government. Granddaddy went to Austin several times to get help on various matters.[16] However, no one in the family seems to remember the name of the person Granddaddy visited. When I started this project, only five of Annie and Dooley's children had survived.

In tracing the origins of this family, I began with the story of Martha Mary's maiden name and the vague story of a man with a wooden leg named Columbus Perkins. These small clues led me on a journey that is still not complete. What we know is that Dooley Wirt Smith was the grandfather of Patricia Ann Waak, Linda Waak Beasley, Roger William Waak and Donald Ray Waak, plus many other of our cousins (photo 12).

While none of us live on the land in the way that Granddaddy's parents and grandparents did, we share a deep, spiritual connection to nature. It is the heritage we were given from him, but it is part of the family soul. We hunger for the simplest of relationships with trees, wind, water, and soil. Even though we all work in different occupations, we share strong ideals and values. Our spiritual practices are ecumenical. My sister is the strongest Baptist, a tradition that dates back at least four generations. One brother reads the Tao as his daily religious practice, and his walking meditations are

---

[15]Johnnie A. Smith, personal Communication. 1998.
[16]Leo Lois Smith Yarber, personal Communication, 1996.

deep mirrors of Creation Spirituality, although he would not call it by that name. My youngest brother has called himself a Christian, a Buddhist, and more recently has followed Native American traditions. He is currently pursuing a master's degree in theology from a Christian seminary.

In the corner of my "living" room is a triangular nook. It contains figures of Eagle, White Buffalo, Bear, and Mouse set in the appropriate directions of east, north, west, and south. Among the figures and the candles I light each day in meditation are small stones, feathers, a bird's nest, pine cones, leaves, a cotton boll, and other symbols of nature. Small framed pictures of Granddaddy and other ancestors sit in among this gathering.

Around the site is an olive bead rosary from Jerusalem, Muslim prayer beads from Egypt, divining stones from Zimbabwe, Buddhist bells from Nepal, and other articles I have collected from my travels around the world. I even have small statues of the goddess that have found their way to this ritual place.

A twelve-foot medicine wheel lies on our land, with each rock brought from some part of the world. On the top of the center rock is a stone that comes from my great-great-grandfather Perkins's cemetery. Each additional rock is placed through ritual to this dedication of sacred space where I honor Earth and the earthly people who sing in our veins.

I am still Christian, but my religious practice embraces a profound spiritual presence that predates all modern religion. Each morning I rise to greet the east and the symbol of the eagle. From here I pray for vision. I turn to the south, the way of the mouse and ask for guidance in my emotional, intuitive life. Then to the west and the symbol of the bear I ask for strength and courage. This direction also includes a request to be present in the world. To the north and the sign of the white buffalo I send out my petition for the best use of my knowledge and that of Earth. To Father Sky I ask for blessing and grace and to Mother Earth I ask to nourish her and be nourished by her.

These prayers come from the Lakota Sioux way, but I also listen to the sounds of nature and ask to never forget the Creation from which I come and that to which I go. It is what my ancestors knew. I believe that this depth of knowledge comes from the bones of those ancestors.

Across a great boundary river
They took their sons and daughters.
These rough and tumble men and women
Were never ones to falter.
She must have wept a thousand times
To leave behind her dear ones.
But grit and dirt and love
Would raise her daughters and her sons.
The cow, the mule, the sheep, the horse,
Those creatures of the land
Were constant, free companions
And always close at hand.
Then one day there were acres
Made for you and me.
The grass, the creek, the wooden house
And rest under a live oak tree.

Chapter 3

Texas Cattle Country

A Texas census identified Martha Perkins living with her parents, Jesse and Lucinda, in Goliad County.[1] It was the first documented evidence of my great-grandmother, and I was absolutely delighted. The next discovery just added to my excitement. Down the road the local schoolteacher, Charles Smith, was boarding with the family of John Cash.[2]

With the beginning of numerous trips down to Goliad, Texas, it did not take much longer to discover a marriage certificate for Charles Smith and Mrs. Martha Quarrels.[3] We knew that Charles had married Martha Perkins on that date. However, it appeared that great-grandmother had been married before to Thomas Quarrells and even had a daughter named Ada. Ada, who no one in the family knew about, appears in the census record where Charles was teaching school.[4]

Having solved that mystery, going backwards in time stumped me. The only names I could find to match Martha's family in previous records were listed as "mulatto."[5] I thought that they could not be the same people because everyone in my family was white, although with an Indian "history." So I immediately discarded these records as unrelated to my search.

To confuse matters more, when I traced the same family names back in time, they were listed on the Louisiana census as "fpc," a new abbreviation for me. In fact, the same family members were listed as "fpc," or as I came

---

[1]U.S. Bureau of the Census, Inhabitants in the County of Goliad County, Texas, 8 August 1870, 89.

[2]Ibid., 91.

[3]Certificate of Marriage for C. W. Smith and Mrs. M. M. Quarrels. Goliad County Courthouse, Goliad TX, 1870.

[4]U.S. Bureau of the Census, Inhabitants in 3rd Precinct, in the County of Callahan, State of Texas, 23 June 1880, 356.

[5]U.S. Bureau of the Census, Houston County, Texas 1850, 367.

to know, "free people of color"[6] in every Louisiana census from 1810 to 1840.[7] In 1850, the Perkins family was classified as "mulatto." Ten years later, the census taker called the same people "Indian."[8] Finally, in the following decade, almost all the same family members were classified as "white."[9]

As the family grew, it was easy to see that one member, Jordan Perkins, was consistently present in each census. So how is the same family group classified by four different ethnic or racial designations over a seventy-year period? Who were these people? In the end the consistency of names and dates convinced me that this family was mine.

One other piece of information came from my mother. Martha Perkins Quarrels Smith was very dark-skinned, according to Granddaddy's sister, Lucretia. As a result, Martha was said to have suffered from intense discrimination. The U.S. census taker in 1880 wrote that Martha Smith's parents came from the "Old Indian Nation." There is even a notation on the record that looks like Rome, Georgia. By this time we had found the records showing Martha's parents' birthplaces as Louisiana. My mother believed that her Grandfather Smith, Martha's husband, told the Old Indian Nation story to explain his wife's skin color. Or perhaps the old family "story" was already in place.

Other researchers have suggested that many of the previous generations indicated they had been born in "Indian Territory" in South Carolina.[10] So how could we recreate the assimilation, or passage, from "colored" to "white" of these family members and discover who, and what, they were?

---

[6]The designation "fpc" or "FPC" occurs in the literature variously as "free *people* of color" and "free *persons* of color," as indeed in the text below.

[7]U.S. Bureau of the Census for Rapides Parish, Louisiana Household Census, 1810, 305; U.S. Bureau of the Census for St. Landry Parish, Louisiana Household Census, 1820, 40; U.S. Bureau of the Census for St. Landry Parish, Louisiana Household Census, 1830, 26; U.S. Bureau of the Census for St. Landry Parish, Louisiana Household Census, 1840, 73.

[8]U.S. Bureau of the Census, Free Inhabitants in Beeville in the County of Bee of Texas, 9 and 10 July 1860, 136.

[9]U.S. Bureau of the Census, Inhabitants in the County of Goliad of Texas, 6 August 1870, 398.

[10]William Duty, personal communication 2001; Joshua Perkins Family Group Sheet, Curtis Jacobs Collection, Sam Houston Regional Library & Research Center, 2003.

I took a course in American genealogy from the National Genealogical Society to add some structure to my research. Tax records seemed to be an excellent follow-up to census rolls. We began the search of every available public record. Texas did not become a state until 1845. Previous records were under the Mexican government and were less accessible. We are still exploring where and how we can locate the records for this time. One possibility, a center set up in Mexico, has yet to be visited.

Although his grandson, Jordan J. Perkins, would claim to have been born in Trinity County, Texas, possibly in 1840, Jordan Perkins of Louisiana was listed in Texas records in 1846. Both he and his son, Jesse, registered for the last Texas poll tax in 1846.[11]

In exploring tax records, Jordan and sons, Jesse and James, paid taxes on their cattle and horses. Jesse owned three horses or mules and eighty-five head of cattle; Jordan had fifteen horses or mules and 250 head of cattle. James, who paid only a poll tax, was probably helping his brother and father keep the stock.[12] It is possible that the men were travelling back and forth across the river between Texas and Louisiana.

The Perkins were not poor by the standards of those days. They had property, which confused the stereotypes of mixed-race people, especially the old story of one drop of African blood making you African. And, of course, all Africans were supposed to be poor. Since these records were also pre-Civil War, the Africans should have been slaves.

A year later, Jesse was not present on the tax rolls. Had he gone off on a cattle drive during the census rounds? Or was he just out in the fields and did not get included? Would his family have been traveling with him? What type of life was riding the cattle trail with your family in tow?

James Perkins had a horse and twenty head of cattle, while father Jordan's stock remained the same. By 1848, Jacob Perkins, another son, had joined Jordan and James. Jordan no longer had horses, but he had added thirty-five sheep to his stock of 250 head of cattle. With 250 head of cattle, I decided that Jordan Perkins was indeed a wealthy man. Jacob and James held twenty-five and thirty-one head of cattle, respectively.[13]

---

[11]Marion Day Mullins, comp., *Republic of Texas: Poll Lists for 1846* (Baltimore: Genealogical Pub. Co., 1974) 132.

[12]Assessment Rolls of Property in Houston County, Texas Tax Records, 1846.

[13]Assessment Rolls of Property in Houston County, Texas Tax Records, 1848.

In 1849, Jesse Perkins had returned to his father's side. He paid taxes on eighty head of cattle while Jordan added sixteen horses and held a total of 300 head of cattle. That seemed to signify a consistent cowherding existence. The two other sons listed no cattle; however, Jacob had three horses. I began to get a picture of the shifting livestock held by cattlemen. Sales would account for the rise and fall of the herd. Some sons may have sold off their cows in the market or been mostly herdsmen for the family members with cattle.[14]

Although all of these men were listed in the 1850 U.S. Census for Houston County, only James Perkins was listed in the tax rolls for the county that year.[15] In these rolls, he was listed as having no property. The remainder of his family seemed to have headed further south. Before following them south, it was important to identify the family members because these were the names that I had to work with over the coming years. Also the names were vital to identification of their racial designation (chart 4).

On November 20, 1850, a Mr. Wortham recorded the household of Jordan Perkins, aged fifty-seven. His occupation was listed as farmer and his place of birth as South Carolina. In his household was Jane Perkins, fifty-five years of age, born also in South Carolina. Enumerated with these two were the following: Hader (Cader) aged twenty-three; Joshua, aged twenty-two; Washington, aged fifteen; and Olive, aged eleven. All of the younger members of the household were identified with Louisiana as their birthplace. All family members were described as being mulatto under the category of color. No other families before or after this page of the census are given a racial designation.[16]

The census taker also enumerated the family of Jesse Perkins several pages later. Jesse was listed as thirty-five years of age and born in Louisiana. Cyndelia, presumably a nickname for Lucinda, was listed as twenty-six years of age, born in Louisiana. The following minor children were listed: Jordan, aged eleven; Martha, aged five; Vianna, aged three; and Keziah, aged four months. The first two children were identified as being born in Louisiana, the second two in Houston County, Texas. If this information is correct, then the family came to Texas between 1845 and 1847. All of the evidence is that they were there by 1846, although they could have migrated back

---

[14]Assessment Rolls of Property in Houston County, Texas Tax Records, 1849.
[15]Assessment Rolls of Property in Houston County, Texas Tax Records, 1850.
[16]U.S. Bureau of the Census for Houston County, Texas, 1850, 367.

and forth across the border. All members of the family are described as mulatto. Once again other families listed in this census record did not have a racial designation noted. Only the Perkins family members were called mulatto.[17]

The U.S. Census also shows that Jacob and James Perkins were living in Houston County at the same time. Close by lived the family of Frederick Bigner. According to the copy of the marriage license obtained from Louisiana, Frederick Bigner had married Charlotta Perkins, daughter of Jordan and "Jinny" Jane Goins. The year 1850 had completed what appeared to be a migration of the known members of this Perkins family. Some members would disperse, but they stayed mostly together over the coming decades.

In 1860, many of the Perkins family reappeared in Bee County, farther south towards the Texas coast.[18] Jesse Perkins was listed as a farmer. In addition to the other children listed, Jesse and Lucinda had added Cader, aged seven; Joshua, aged four; and James M. aged one. (According to my grandfather, Joshua had a twin brother, Jesse. There are no records to prove this; however, there is a Texas mortality record showing the death of a child named Jesse Perkins about the same time.)

Jesse's son, Jordan, lived with a "laborer," Jesse Carter. Farmer Washington Perkins and his wife Elizabeth headed the next household. Next to Washington, lived Jordan and Jane Perkins, now sixty-seven and sixty-five years old, respectively.

Bill Dyer, aged twenty-seven, headed the next household. He was listed as a laborer. He lived with his wife, Olive. The next household was headed by a farmer, Josiah (Jacob, as far as we can tell) Perkins. His wife Mary was followed by these children: Isaac, aged eighteen; Caroline, aged sixteen; Sarah, aged fourteen; Joshua, aged ten; Laura E., aged eight; Jesse, aged five; and Cader, aged two.

The next household enumerated a farmer, Joshua Perkins, with a wife, Amanda; and a daughter, Allie, ten months old. A thirty-three-year-old farmer, Cader Perkins, occupied the last household in this grouping. This completion of a block of households headed by names of various children from the 1850 U.S. census suggests that the family was together in Bee

---

[17]Ibid., 367.

[18]U.S. Bureau of the Census, Inhabitants in Beeville in the County of Bee of Texas, 9 and 10 July 1860, 44-45.

County, with the exception of James Perkins and Frederic and Charlotta Bigner.

However, the most distinctive characteristic revealed in this census is once again the designation of race. While none of the other families before or after the Perkins group list a racial description, the Perkins family had one. With the exception of Bill Dyer and his wife, Olive, all Perkins family members and the laborer Jesse Carter are labeled as "Indians." Future racial differentials disappeared, but this Indian story would stay with the family through the generations to come.

Goliad County, Texas records indicate that Jesse and Lucinda Perkins were living in the area ten years later. In their household were twenty-five-year-old Martha, twenty-year-old Keziah, and seventeen-year-old Kader.[19] In addition, the names of Joshua, James and Beauregard were included as children (see chart 5). Vianna Perkins had married John Rice and lived in the Goliad area. Jesse's son, Jordan, had married Margaret Taylor. They were living in a nearby county.[20] The other children of Jordan and Jane Perkins also appear in the documents for the same area.

However, father, Jordan and mother, Jane, had disappeared from the census rolls by 1870. Their son, Cader, was living in the household of Amanda Earl. Seven children were listed, ranging from fifteen years of age to six months. I would later discover that there was a great deal of confusion about whether Cader was the father of some or all of these children. The more pertinent issue is that all the Perkins family members are designated as "white" in the color category. That remained the case in the 1880 U.S. Census, with the exception of Beauregard who was called mulatto again.

The reconstructed Texas family included Jordan and "Jinny" or Jane Perkins as the parents of Jesse, Charlotta, Jacob or Josiah, James, Washington, Cader, Joshua and Olive. Lewis P. Dykes married Charlotte Bigner before 1860 so Charlotta's husband, Frederic, must have died in those first years in Texas.[21] Charloty Dykes was living next to or with Thomas Dykes, her stepson among the Perkins family in Goliad by 1880. In her household

---

[19]U.S. Bureau of the Census, Inhabitants in the County of Goliad, Texas, 8 August 1870, 89.

[20]U.S. Bureau of the Census, Inhabitants of Precinct 5 of the County of DeWitt of Texas, August 1870, 17.

[21]Kaye Hancock, personal Communication 1998.

were another daughter-in-law, Narcissa Bigner, aged thirty-one, and two granddaughters Janey, aged thirteen, and Elizabeth, aged eight.[22]

Olive Perkins was married to Bill Dyer in 1860.[23] However, in subsequent years, Olive lived with one or another of her brothers keeping house. She was either deserted by her husband or left a widow. No children were ever recorded. However, the relationship of the family was further reinforced by the repetitive names of Jordan, Jesse, Joshua, Olive, and Cader.

Records from Beeville Precinct give evidence of the Perkins family's arrival in this part of the country. The records also underscore their overall wealth. Jesse Perkins owned nine horses, five milk cows, ten swine, and 300 head of cattle. Jordan Perkins was the owner of seventy-five acres of undeveloped land, thirteen horses, four milk cows, 500 head of cattle. Jacob Perkins had one horse, three milk cows, six working oxen, and twenty head of cattle. Josh Perkins had two horses, a milk cow, three working oxen, and five swine.[24]

The tax records help delineate the timing of when the family moved from place to place. Jesse Perkins was taxed in Bee County, Texas in 1860.[25] Jordan and Joshua Perkins appeared on the tax rolls, along with Jesse, from 1861 to 1864. In 1864, Jesse appeared to own 200 acres of a St. John Jones land grant. His father, Jordan, had acquired one hundred acres of land under the same grant.[26] In 1865, a Mrs. E. L. Perkins and W. B. (Washington) Perkins as taxpayers join Jordan and Joshua Perkins. Mrs. E. L. Perkins could be Lucinda, based on later tax records where she kept her husband's land. Jesse is not listed, so one might presume that he was on a cattle drive at tax time.[27]

In 1866, Mrs. E. L. Perkins is not listed, but Jordan, W. B., and Joshua Perkins did pay their taxes.[28] The following year Joshua had left, leaving the taxes to Jordan and W. B. In 1868, W. B. Perkins alone paid taxes, and in

---

[22]U.S. Bureau of the Census, Inhabitants in Commissioners Precinct No. 2, Goliad County, 22 and 23 June 1880, 351.

[23]U.S. Bureau of the Census, Bee County 1860, 44.

[24]U.S. Bureau of the Census, Productions of Agriculture in Beeville Precinct in the County of Bee in the Post Office of Beeville, 1860, 11.

[25]Assessment of Property Situated in Bee County TX for 1860.

[26]Assessment of Property Situated in Bee County TX for 1864.

[27]Assessment of Property Situated in Bee County TX for 1865.

[28]Assessment of Property Situated in Bee County TX for 1866.

1869, he was rejoined by Joshua Perkins.[29] Jordan probably died between 1867 and 1868 because he is never listed again in any census or land records.

However, in 1869, Jesse Perkins appeared in Goliad County as the tax-payer for 160 acres of a Pedro Villa land grant and two horses.[30] It is possible he had moved into Goliad, the adjoining county, as early as 1866. However, I have found no records that show this. The county lines changed at some point during the period. Cader Perkins reappeared near his brother Jesse the following year in Goliad as the owner of four horses and fifteen head of cattle.[31]

Mrs. Lucinda Perkins paid the taxes on the 160 acres in 1871.[32] By 1874 she had added what looks like eight horses and eighty head of cattle. Her brother-in-law, W. B. Perkins, was also the owner of 160 acres and had eighteen horses and eighty head of cattle. In 1876, Lucinda's acreage had moved over to another land grant, and Joshua Perkins owned 160 acres of Pedro Villa. At this point it is confusing as to whether this Joshua was Lucinda and Jesse's son or Jesse's brother. In addition, a new Perkins land-owner appears. Henry Perkins also paid taxes on 160 acres of the Pedro Villa land grant.[33]

The name of Henry Perkins turned up in various records relating to later trouble with Jesse and Lucinda's sons, Cader, Joshua and James. There seemed to be various accusations of livestock theft. Henry was cleared but the three boys along with a cousin were sent to jail.[34] Two years ago I made

---

[29]Assessment of Property Situated in Bee County TX for 1867, 1868, 1869.

[30]Assessment Roll of the County of Goliad for Ad Valorem Income and Salary Tax for 1869, 15.

[31]Assessment Roll of the County of Goliad for Ad Valorem Income and Salary Tax for 1870, 13-14.

[32]Assessment Roll of the County of Goliad for Ad Valorem Income and Salary Tax for 1871, 26.

[33]Assessment Roll of the County of Goliad for Ad Valorem Income and Salary Tax for 1874, 19.

[34]The *State of Texas vs. Henry Perkins et. al.*, case 1244., 1878. Henry Perkins and the Perkins boys (James, Joshua, and Cato) were accused of stealing six hogs. The accusers never appeared to testify in court and the case was dropped. However, in the *State of Texas vs. Cato Perkins, James Perkins, Joshua Perkins, & Alex Linney*, case 1280, 1879, the young men were indicted for the theft of ten mules. Cato, James, and Joshua were the sons of Lucinda and Jesse Perkins. Alex Linney was the

contact with one of Henry's descendants. According to him, Henry was the son of Jesse's brother James. He married Rebecca Rice, the sister of John Rice, Vianna Perkins's husband.[35]

The same situation remained in 1877, with the addition of Cade Perkins to the tax rolls and his ownership of a horse. Since he was enumerated separately from the others, he could have been living in town or on another property. This Cade (or Cader) could have been Jesse's son or brother. The brother was living with Amanda Earle at that time. Cader Perkins and Amanda appeared in court under the charge of living together without being married. They finally did marry in 1873, and charges were dropped.[36]

In 1878 and 1879, Joshua Perkins paid the taxes on 150 acres of Pedro Villa land. There is no further mention of Lucinda Perkins in any tax or census records. My assumption is that she died sometime in this period, although we have not discovered any death records or cemetery plots. In 1878, Joshua, W. B., Henry, and Cado Perkins were listed as taxpayers.[37] Since Cado was the name used by Jesse's son, he may have taken over his mother's duties.

In addition, a new name appeared. Edward, or Ed, Perkins appeared in the records for the first time. In 1878, he was listed as a "f.m.c." or free

---

grandson of W. B. Perkins. Despite not-guilty pleas, the jury found them guilty and, on 31 May 1879, sentenced them to seven years in the penitentiary. On 2 June 1879, court records show the four men were ordered to move to the DeWitt County Jail because of unhealthy conditions in Goliad. All four were received in the Huntsville, Texas State Prison on 17 January 1880. On 2 February 1880 they lost an appeal to their conviction. Alex Linney escaped in August 1880. Both Jim and Joshua escaped the following year. Cato was pardoned after four years but, more than a year later, ended up at Rusk State Penitentiary for stealing horses and personal property. He was pardoned again in 1890. It appears from records that he was a respectable farmer thereafter until his death. The prison records describe each individual as having dark complexion, black hair, and either black or hazel eyes. They also give height and weight, as well as other pertinent information. See *Convict Record Ledgers* (1849–1954), nos. 8389, 8390, 8391, 8392, 311, 2176, Texas State Archives.

[35]Brian Rick, personal Communication, 2000.

[36]Assessment of Property Situated in the County of Goliad TX, 1877 & Goliad Court Records, 1873.

[37]Assessment of Property Situated in the County of Goliad TX, 1878.

man of color. To date I have not been able to identify his relationship to the family members. An individual named Ed Perkins appeared in the U.S. census of Callahan County, Texas at the same time as Martha Perkins and Charles Smith.[38] His first daughter is named Martha M., and he has been identified as the son of James Perkins, Jesse's brother.

In 1880, J. H. Perkins, who will later be identified as Joshua H. Perkins, joined Joshua, W. B., and Henry. Joshua H. Perkins, with his wife, Manda (Amanda), made a land transaction with one of the largest landowners in the area. Joshua and Amanda bought one piece of land and sold another in the general area of Sarco Creek in Goliad County.[39] Joshua H. was the son of Jordan Perkins and Jenny Goins, according to his death certificate in 1912.[40] The other Joshua listed as a taxpayer may have been the son of Jesse and Lucinda.

The Perkins continued to pay taxes on land and cattle into the 1890s. Today one Perkins family still lives in the Sarco Creek area. But as this story began to unravel, we were unable to contact anyone in the area except an elderly wife of a Perkins descendant. She said that her husband's parents had separated when he was small, and she did not have any information about his father's family.

Like many counties in the South, a bound volume of Goliad's history was available from the county historical commission. In the book there is very little reported about the Perkins family. However one page held a small item of information for our investigation. The paragraph made reference to an old cemetery located across Sarco Creek on the Laurence Wood Ranch.[41] According to the account, Jessie Perkins was buried there. He had been killed "running Gaucho." The paragraph went on to explain that "running Gaucho" involved "hanging a rustler up by the legs, riding on a horse and pulling his head off." It did not explain whether Jessie was the rider or the rustler. However, Mrs. Jeanette Perkins, the elderly widow, told me in a

---

[38]Assessment of Property Situated in the County of Goliad TX, 1878–1880; U.S. Census for Callahan County, Texas, 1880.

[39]Deed Records for Goliad County TX, V/495/497, 8 July 1893.

[40]Death Certificate 0116 for Joshua Perkins, 1912. Texas State Department of Health: Bureau of Vital Statistics.

[41]Jakie L. Pruett and Everett B. Cole, eds., *The History and Heritage of Goliad County* (Austin TX: Eakin Publications, 1983) 253.

phone conversation that Jesse Perkins was an accomplished roper, and he had a grandson who was a champion roper.

Most important was a growing image of stockkeepers, ropers, cattlemen, and ultimately the legendary Texas cowboy. Whether the Perkins family had adopted cattle raising as their occupation of choice, or cattle rearing was part of their culture and heritage throughout the generations, cattle as a business and lifestyle became the mainstay of their existence. The leading historians of cattle ranching in North America point to triracial cowboys as the transporters of this way of life to the west.[42]

As white settlers opened Texas, other ethnic groups saw opportunities in the state as well. The Ashworth family moved into east Texas in the 1830s.[43] Two of Jordan Perkins's sisters had married into the Ashworth clan in Louisiana and the Ashworths were generally accepted as triracial, although black Western historians claim the Ashworths as "black cowboy(s)."[44] A researcher states that "one member of the previously mentioned Ashworth clan, a 'red bone' family of mixed white-black-Indian ancestry, owned far more cattle than anyone else in Jefferson County in 1850."[45] Texas was an acceptable place for a mixed-race group to prosper, given the local residence of Native Americans and Mexicans. Also moving in a group to the frontier provided freedom for the Perkins and other triracial families.

Goliad was not only good cattle country; it became the home for the Perkins for decades. Discovering the Goliad historical records included the cemetery records. Texas was not required to keep birth and death records until 1906. As a result, hours were spent in the Goliad County Courthouse. Unfortunately, the courthouse had experienced a fire in 1870, so many records were lost.

The library and historical commission became other sources of information. The local cemeteries had been listed in a loose-leaf book written many years earlier. We were able to easily access the cemetery at Sarco Creek, the community where most of the family had lived (photo 13). None of the original Perkins family members were listed as buried there.

---

[42]Terry G. Jordan, *North American Cattle-Ranching Frontiers* (Albuquerque: University of New Mexico Press, 1993) 117.

[43]Terry G. Jordan, *Trails to Texas* (Lincoln: University of Nebraska, 1981) 64.

[44]Philip Durham and Everett L. Jones, *The Negro Cowboys* (Lincoln: University of Nebraska Press, 1965) 17-18.

[45]Jordan, *Trails to Texas*, 78.

However, we found death certificates for Joshua Perkins and his wife, Amanda, who died in 1912 and 1914, respectively. Joshua's death certificate listed his parents as Jordan Perkins and Jenny Jane Goen. There are two unmarked graves among the Perkins plots at Sarco Creek and both death certificates stated that they were being buried at Sarco Creek Cemetery. Although the cemetery book did not list a grave for Washington Perkins, the death certificate for 1916 stated that he was being buried in Sarco Creek Cemetery.[46] When we arrived, we found a fairly new marker for Washington Perkins in the cemetery. The death certificate made reference to his father being born in Georgia. We knew Washington was a son of Jordan Perkins born in South Carolina; however, once again the reference to Georgia was made. This second reference joined that of the 1880 census taker. What was the connection to Georgia?

The only other information found in public records besides land ownership, censuses, and death certificates for W. B. Perkins was his request for a Civil War pension. In 1910, he stated that he was seventy-five years old and had been born in Calcasue [*sic*] Parish, Louisiana. He also stated that he had been in Texas for about sixty-five years.[47] If he was correct, then his parents had been living in Calcasieu Parish in 1835 and had arrived with their families in Texas around 1845.

J. J. or Jordan Perkins, the son of Jesse, also applied for Civil War pension. He stated that his full name was Jerry Jourdan Perkins.[48] (There seem to be several variations on the spelling of Jordan.) He claimed to be seventy-six years of age and to have been born in Trinity County, Texas. All the prior censuses have him born in Louisiana, but this raised the question of whether the family moved back and forth across the border between Texas and Louisiana. We knew they came from the "Neutral Zone" between the two states so maybe there was confusion about what state they were living in.

Also the question was raised that if he were born in 1838, his mother, Lucinda, would have been fourteen years old. Of course, the theory of Lucinda's age also was off, with variations in her age at each census. Ages and birth dates aside, there were several pieces of evidence that seemed to

[46]Death Certificate 0117 for Washington Perkins, 1916. Texas State Department of Health: Bureau of Vital Statistics.

[47]Confederate Pension Application, W. B. Perkins, 2947. Texas State Archives.

[48]Confederate Pension Application, J. J. Perkins, 27543. Texas State Archives.

underline this Jerry Jordan as my great-grandmother's brother. First, J. J. Perkins registered to vote with Charles Smith at the Goliad County Courthouse in 1872. The document shows that they went to the courthouse together and actually signed in one after the other.[49] The only other Perkins to register was W. B., but he was not accompanied by either J. J. or Charles. It would make sense that brothers-in-law would associate with each other.

Second, there is the family story about a cousin with a wooden leg. When I first heard the story, it seemed too preposterous to believe. However, my mother told the story and so did my aunt and uncle.[50] In the 1920s, Granddaddy's first cousin, Columbus Perkins, came to visit the family. He stayed for a while and helped them chop cotton. Each of the family members recalled that he had a wooden branch that he rested his knee in because of a mangled lower leg.

I found a census record of Jordan Perkins living in a boarding house with his son, Columbus. Next to the boarding house lived Boash Perkins and Charles Bundick.[51] This same Charles Bundick would sign an affidavit that enabled Columbus Perkins to get a birth certificate in 1947.[52] In 1996, I located a son of Charles Bundick, also named Charles Bundick. He describes his first cousin as follows.

> My father never talked that much about this parents but he did come from DeWitt County and Columbus Perkins was his cousin. Columbus used to visit our house in Pledger, Texas fairly often in the 1940's. He had a terrific sense of humor and usually walked wherever he went. I was in my early teens at that time (I was born in 32). When Columbus was a child he got his lower leg caught in some sort of gear train that left him crippled from his knee down. I believe it was his left leg that was crippled but it didn't slow him down that much. He worked in a gasoline service station about 8 miles south of Pledger. At that time we called it Merrit's corner. It was located at the intersection of the road that runs from Bay City to West Columbia and the road running south from Pledger. Columbus made his own wooden leg from the fork of an oak tree limb. He had a leather pad

---

[49]List of Registered Voters of Goliad County, State of Texas, 1872, 23.

[50]Nell Waak, Pearl Smith Doherty, and Dooley W. Smith, Jr., personal communications, 1998.

[51]U.S. Bureau of the Census, DeWitt County Texas Household Census, 1900, 28.

[52]Certificate of Birth for Columbus F. Perkins 5643, 1947. Texas Department of Health: Bureau of Vital Statistics.

filled with cotton that his knee rested on in the fork of the limb. One branch of the limb was cut off about 3 inches above the pad and the other branch ran up and tied into a wide belt around his waist. He was a very happy person who laughed all the time.[53]

Much of this information would be verified when I encountered a new cousin, Shirley Conrad, in 1999. Shirley is the granddaughter of Columbus Perkins. She not only had his history, but pictures of him and a picture of Jordan Perkins, his father (photos 14, 15, and 16).

So who was the original Charles Bundick? And how did he relate to this family? On May 15, 1871, C. E. [Charles] Bundick married K. Z. [Keziah] Perkins in Goliad County, Texas.[54] Keziah was the daughter of Jesse and Lucinda Perkins. She gave birth to a son, the second Charles Bundick, before her husband died. After C. E.'s death, Keziah married William Jacob [Jake] Bundick, Charles's brother. Keziah and Jake were found in the 1880 U.S. census for Goliad County and in the agricultural production census of that time. In a listing for the old Laurence Wood Cemetery, there were several Bundick graves.

In 1997, my husband and I finally received permission to enter Laurence Wood's private land to look for the old cemetery. We found the cemetery in an isolated portion of the pasture. It has essentially been abandoned; however, at the southern entrance to a motte, or grove, of trees there is a line of marked and unmarked graves. My mother, my husband, and I were led to the cemetery situated among live oaks by Chris Bush, husband of Shannon Wood, one of the owners (photo 17).

We found the grave of Keziah Perkins Bundick, born February 7, 1852 and died March 2, 1882 (photo 18). Her descendants know little about her. The Goliad cemetery book lists fifteen graves close to the banks of Sarco Creek.[55] Elizabeth Perkins, wife of W. B., is buried within a rusty iron fence. Keziah Perkins Bundick is just outside the fence. There are at least two gravesites on the other side where the stones are worn down to just beneath the ground. There may be one or two other graves inside the fence.

---

[53]Charles Bundick, personal correspondence, 1996.
[54]Certificate of Marriage for C. E. Bundick and K. Z. Perkins. Goliad County Courthouse, 1871.
[55]Rosemarie Bammert, ed., *Cemetery Listings of Goliad County, Texas* (Goliad TX: Goliad County Historical Commission, 1988) 116.

However, unrecorded, except by someone's faint memory, is a grave on the right side of Keziah. The stone had been pushed up out of the ground and was resting against the trunk of a live oak tree. On its face is the following inscription:

IN MEMORY OF
JESSEY
Husband of Lucinda
PERKINS
Born Feb. 17 1816
Died Jan. 7 1871

I had found the resting place of my great-great-grandfather (photo 19). How appropriate: he was buried under a live oak on the bank of a flowing stream in the middle of a cow pasture.

After wandering across the state in search of records and digging into dusty archives, we found this moss-covered, worn piece of rock that gave us more information than any piece of paper. My mother was stunned. As far as she knew, no one in the family even knew Jesse Perkins's name, much less where he lived, died, and was buried. I yearned to be able to take her to her grandmother's grave, but this moment was a landmark in itself. We were recovering the family, page by page, rock by rock.

We do not know where Jesse's eldest daughter, my great-grandmother, is buried. We do not know where Jesse's parents are interred. We do not know where Lucinda's remains rest, but we now believe that we know Lucinda's maiden name.

Sometime after making contact with a present-day Charles Bundick, descendant of Keziah Perkins Bundick, he urged me to talk with his brother, Howard. Rev. Howard Bundick is a retired Baptist minister living in south Texas. When I finally called Rev. Bundick, we had a wonderful conversation about the family history I was gathering and all the information that was still missing. He remarked that his father had become estranged from the Bundick family after Keziah died. Apparently there was competition between two Bundick half-brothers. So Keziah's son, Charles, left home. It seems apparent from the records that he went to live and work with his maternal cousins, the Perkins, because he appeared on the census in DeWitt County, Texas living with Boash Perkins, a brother of Columbus.

I asked Rev. Bundick about any history of Indian heritage. His answer mirrored the stories I had heard in my own family. Yes, there were stories in his family that his grandmother was an American Indian. Rev. Bundick said that his skin was very dark, and his sons and grandsons were very dark-skinned. When Rev. Bundick asked his father why their skin was so dark, his father said they were part Indian from the grandmother's side.

As a final question, I asked Rev. Bundick whether he had ever heard the maiden name of his father's grandmother. He answered, yes, she was a Willis. His father assumed she was named after some Willis families who were Indian. A Willis family had founded Willis, Texas, and he assumed they were the same people.[56] However, I knew the answer even before I verified the fact that she was not from the family for which Willis, Texas was named. I knew where Lucinda Willis came from, and I was stunned.

---

[56]Rev. Howard Bundick, personal communication, 1999.

We are bound for no man's land
Where they say that we will be free.
We are bound for the promised land
Where we can really be.

My children will sing;
They will dance and play.
We will follow the river
And praise the day

That we came to no man's land
And were left to make our way.

Chapter 4

The Neutral Zone

The migration of the Perkins family paralleled that of a number of associated other families who traveled from Tennessee and the Carolinas into Louisiana at the close of the century. Two "Joshua Perkins" families were listed in the 1800 U.S. census for Buncombe County, North Carolina. One is listed as a "free man of color."[1] There is considerable confusion over which Joshua Perkins was the father of which family in later generations, but the racial designation did not change for the Joshua Perkins who was settled in Louisiana at the time of the 1810 Opelousas, Louisiana Federal Census.

Various descendants describe how Reverend Joseph Willis brought a group of families west with him in the late 1700s to early 1800s. Reverend Willis's story is recounted later because I believe he is also a relative and may be the source of the Cherokee-wife legend in my family. The families of Sweat, Perkins, and others accompanied Willis into Louisiana and settled primarily in Rapides and St. Landry Parishes. The families stayed together and intermarried within a large community of "free people/persons of color" with the surnames of Ashworth, Goins, Dial, Nash, Bass, Ivey, Bunch, and Groves.

The movement west was probably part of the continued pioneering spirit of citizens of the United States during the early days of independence from Europe. However, the Perkins and other mixed-race families seemed to live on the edge of established social norms by virtue of their color. And Louisiana offered many opportunities that the eastern Southern states did not. First, there was a long history of tolerance for "free people of color." James Pitot, a French businessman, makes reference to "free people of color"

---

[1]U.S. Bureau of the Census, Buncombe County Household Census of North Carolina, 1800. 83.

and their participation in the life of the Louisiana Colony in memoirs he kept from 1796 to 1802.[2]

Another historian describes the existence of the group, called *gens de couleur libre*, in early Louisiana.[3] Although his work is primarily focused on Creoles of color, this researcher lays out some important guidelines for the study of mixed-race people, especially in early Louisiana. Early records included classifications such as Negro (full-blooded); Sacatra (seven-eighths Negro and one-eighth white); Griffe (three-quarters Negro and one-quarter white); Mulatto (one-half Negro and one-half white); Quadroon (one-quarter Negro and three-quarters white); and Octoroon/sang-mele (one-eighth Negro and seven-eighths white).[4]

The designations are probably meaningless in terms of the Perkins family and their associated clan members. However, the Perkins, Willis, Ashworth, Goins, Sweat, and Nash families did intermarry quite frequently during the Louisiana years. Historians Virginia DeMarce and Gary Mills have identified all of these names with the triracial grouping. In studies of the Creoles of Cane River, Louisiana, the author states that free families of color tended to stay together and intermarry. Certainly they did not have to face opposition by their families for marrying a person of color or white, as both earlier and later generations did.

A second reason for the appeal of Louisiana was the ability to be outside the realm of traditional law and mores. This point may seem at odds with the tendency on the part of Perkins and Sweats to engage in lawsuits. However, in the beginning they lived in what has been called the "Neutral Zone," "Neutral Strip," or "No-Man's-Land." In 1803 there was no established boundary between the United States (as a result of the Louisiana Purchase) and Spain, which then held what we know of today as Texas. As soon as the U.S. government took over the Louisiana Territory, Spanish soldiers were sent to hold the border.[5]

---

[2]James Pitot, *Observations on the Colony of Louisiana from 1792 to 1802* (Baton Rouge: Louisiana State University Press, 1979) 11, 29, 114.

[3]Gary B. Mills, *The Forgotten People: Cane River's Creoles of Color* (Baton Rouge: Louisiana University Press, 1977) xiii.

[4]Mills, *The Forgotten People*, xiii-xiv.

[5]Carolyn Ericson, *Natchitoches Neighbors in the Neutral Strip: Land Claims between the Rio Hondo and the Sabine* (Nacogdoches TX: Ericson Books, 1993) iii.

Spain and the United States reached an agreement to establish a neutral area between the Sabine River and the Arroyo Hondo River. The Arroyo Hondo would later be called the Rio Hondo, the Calcasieu, or Quelqueshoe. Ownership of the land in this area would not be established until 1824 and then ratified by the Louisiana House of Representatives in 1836.[6] Thus, for a period of roughly twenty years, the area was open for settlement.

One account written in the 1930s and reprinted from a manuscript suggests that the Neutral Zone was perfect for people who wanted to disappear. Webster Talma Crawford, stated that much of the less-desirable elements of society found their way to the area.

> Escaped criminals, whom the officers of the law had no intention of following, bandits, runaway slaves, vagabond French traders with their Indian concubines, English traders ditto, and others unclassified; men from God-Knows-Where flocked to this genuine no-man's-land, between the Quelqueshoe and the Rio Sabinas. This was the period of incubation of the Redbone [*sic*]; and the environment in which he grew.[7]

Whether Crawford's characterization is close to the facts or just another evidence of prejudice against racially mixed people can be left to anyone's guess. However, other comments that he makes in his manuscript suggest the latter. In any case, the existence of a lawless area available for land ownership and cattle ranching would be an appealing settlement area for the Perkins family. In fact, a claim was made in this area by Hiram Ours, which stated that he had received the tract of land through a chain of transfers from Jordan Perkins.[8]

The third reason for the move to Louisiana rests on the force and charisma of Reverend Joseph Willis. I have devoted a separate chapter to Rev. Willis because of the extraordinary circumstances around his life. He had been born a slave and was of mixed-race parentage, although there is a great deal of dispute around what those races might be. He also was a Baptist minister and had been encouraged to come west to preach the gospel. Willis had clear links to the Perkins family. All the histories have

[6]Ericson, *Natchitoches Neighbors in the Neutral Strip*, 1.

[7]Webster Talma Crawford, *The Cherry Winche Country: Origins of the Red Bones: and, the Westport Fight*, ed. Don C. Marler and Jane P. McManus (Woodville TX: Dogwood Press, 1993) 21.

[8]Ericson, *Natchitoches Neighbors in the Neutral Strip*, 137.

stated that he came to Louisiana looking for a man named Perkins.[9] Willis arrived in Louisiana in the early 1800s and would live out his life in Louisiana. Most of the families who came with him would either stay in Louisiana for generations or move across the border to Texas. The Willis family intermarried with these families.

Whatever the reason, the Perkins family made Louisiana their home as well. A characterization of that life is found in various legal records in the state. For example, Joshua Perkins brought a wife with him to the state. We know her name was Mary Mixon because she and her husband signed the marriage bond for their daughter, Sarah Perkins, to marry Jesse Ashworth on October 2, 1810.[10] Additional daughters included Mary Perkins, who married James Ashworth and Elizabeth Perkins, who married James Goings (or Goins).[11] My great-great-great-grandfather, Jordan Perkins, married Virginia Jane (Jinny) Goen (or Goins) on March 12, 1814.[12] Joshua Perkins signed the bond for this marriage as well.

There may have been additional children of Joshua and Mary Perkins, including Lucy Perkins, who married Arville Rogers, and Cader Perkins, who married Elizabeth Hoozer (see chart 6). Since Lucy was born in South Carolina the year before Sarah, she is possibly the oldest of Joshua and Mary's children. Cader would have been born roughly two years after Jordan. He was also married three years after Jordan's marriage to Jane Goins and the name Cader appeared for several generations after in Jordan's descendants.

However, the relationship is most clear with Sarah, Mary, Elizabeth, and Jordan because years later they became locked in a legal battle over Joshua's estate. Mary was married to James Ashworth; Sarah married James's brother, Jesse Ashworth. Elizabeth Perkins had married Virginia Goen Perkins's brother, James Goings. (Various spellings existed for the Goins's family.)

---

[9]Randy Willis, personal communication, 2000; Sandra Loridans, personal communication, 1999; Erbon Wise, personal communication, 1999.

[10]Certificate of Marriage 14 for Sarah Perkins & Jesse Ashworth, 1810. St. Landry Parish Courthouse, Opelousas LA.

[11]In the records, the family name occurs variously as Goins, Goings, and even Goen, Gowens, and Gawain.

[12]Certificate of Marriage 9 for Jordan Perkins & Virginia Goen, 1814. St. Landry Parish Courthouse, Opelousas LA.

Several years before Joshua had testified in his friend Gilbert Sweat's court battle. Because both cases were clearly struggles over property and provide information about relationships, they are transcribed in detail. These cases provide important data on the racial origin and lifestyle of the people involved. Each case lists some of the evidence about the family that was helpful in tracing the origins of individuals and their destinations. As in all of the court cases and testimony transcribed for this book, the text has been edited for grammar and clarity, unless there is something of value in quoting directly. The court transcripts are presented in italics; editorial comments are in brackets and in roman type.

Mary Perkins, et al. vs. Joshua Perkins
Court of Probate
Parish of St. Landry
Opelousas, Louisiana

To the Honorable the Judge of the Court of Probate acting in and for the Parish of St. Landry

The petition of Mary Perkins, wife of James Ashworth, who authorizes this suit and joins his said wife herein, of Sarah Perkins, wife of Jesse Ashworth, who authorizes this suit and joins his wife herein and of Elizabeth Perkins, wife of James Goings, who authorizes this suit and joins his said wife herein, and of said persons being free persons of color and residing in the Parish of St. Landry where the have their legal domicile respectfully showeth;

That Joshua Perkins, free man of color, father of your petitioners, is a very old man and has become so infirm and helpless as to be incapable of taking care of his person and administering his estate;

That the infirmities of said Joshua Perkins are extreme old age and total blindness;

That he has considerable property which is liable to be wasted and he is in danger of being reduced to want in his old age unless a curator be approved to take care of his person & property.

The premises considered, your petitioners pray that the said Joshua Perkins may be regularly and legally interdicted, and that a curator be legally appointed to take care of his person and administer his estate;

That the said Joshua Perkins may be cited, as the law directs, to appear and answer this petition and to show cause, if any he have or can, why he should not be interdicted and a curator appointed for him.

They pray for all other and further relief, in the finances, that law and equity will allow. Signed by Thomas H. Serris, Attorney for Petitioners
Filed 15 June 1837 with Robert Taylor, Clerk.

Testimony

Mary Perkins et al	}	No. 149 Court of Probates
vs	}	St Landry
Joshua Perkins	}	

William Neyland, being duly sworn, states that he knows Joshua Perkins, Defendant in the above suit. He has known him for about 12 or 15 years. He [Perkins] is very infirm. He believes him to be almost entirely blind. He may see a little but very little, if any. He cannot see sufficiently to read, if he ever could. Witness never knew him to read or write. He does not know how long the Defendant has been blind, or nearly so, but that he has been in that situation about two years. He cannot see how to walk about the house during that time, and he has to make use of a stick to feel his way. Witness does not think Defendant is in a situation to transact any business at all. From his knowledge of Defendant's situation, he knows that he could not take any steps himself to prevent his property being dissipated and wasted. Witness stated himself that Defendant told him about 2 weeks earlier that he was not capable of managing his own business.

He is in the habit of seeing the Defendant frequently. He thinks that his mind is not sound. He does not know if his property is being wasted. He is not able to say whether or not his property has decreased since it is principally cattle, and he has not been among them. He thinks him [the Defendant] childish but he sometimes talks rationally on ordinary subjects. He does not speak wild but has very little presence of mind about him. His memory is bad. He thinks it the loss of mind from old age that decays the mind with the body. He commenced a conversation with Deponent about 2 weeks earlier about the suit, and he told him that he was not capable of attending to his business.
He is between 70 to 80 years of age.
Sworn & Subscribed this 19th March   William Neyland
1838 before Mr. Robert Taylor, Justice Peace, St. Landry

George Perkins, being duly sworn, says that deponent is 52 years and had known the Defendant as long as he has recollection of anybody. [George may have been Joshua's son by a first marriage. However, there is no proof of this except for a family sheet in the Curtis Jacobs Collection.] The Defendant is blind. He has told Deponent that he cannot discern daylight from darkness. He has been getting blind for the last three years. He has been totally incapable for that time of doing any business. He is very old and very infirm. He is about 80 years of age. He [the Deponent] has been in the habit of seeing the Defendant for the last four or five years. He is a neighbor and lives within

*four or five miles of him. He does not know whether his property has increased
or diminished. He does not know of any of his property's having been wasted.
His cattle are put in the hands of Charles Trahan by Jordan Perkins, who
transacts his business generally. His property consists chiefly of cattle. It is
generally the way to manage them by putting them in the hands of a vacherie
keeper. Mr. Trahan has been considered a good manager of stock, but the
witness thinks that he is getting too old now. He does not think that he is
capable of managing them.*

  Sworn & Subscribed to George X Perkins
  This 19th March 1838 [The X is his mark]
  Before Mr. Robert Taylor, Justice of the Peace, St. Landry

Mary Perkins et al   Probate Court Parish of St. Landry
   vs   No. 149
Joshua Perkins

  *Testimony taken by consent of parties subject to all legal exceptions.
Hardy Coward, witness for Plaintiffs, sworn testimony:
He knows Joshua Perkins, the Defendant, to be blind. He can distinguish
daylight. He confessed to witness that he distinguishes day from night with
difficulty. He finds his way with a stick or is led about. The witness is well
acquainted with the Defendant, who never knows witness, except by the sound
of his voice. A long and intimate acquaintance has existed between the two,
even before the blindness of Defendant. He believes the Defendant to be from
eighty to eighty-four years of age. It has been 55 or 56 years since he was a
grown man. The Defendant was in the military service of the U.S. during the
Revolutionary War and was then a grown man. The witness is sixty-two years
old. The Defendant enjoys good health and possesses his usual strength and
activity. He is not infirm. He is as strong and hearty as most men of his age.
He thinks his mind has been weakened by age, and he can not manage his
affairs without assistance. He thinks if Defendant could see, he would be able
to manage his business. He can ride horseback. From the loss of recollection, he
might be liable to be imposed on. Some time since the Witness had paid five
hundred dollars to the Defendant. He thinks he might have paid him only a
part without his even detecting the deception. The money was the proceeds of
notes left in witness's hands for collection by Jordan Perkins, son of the
Defendant. He does not know that any part of the Defendant's property has
been wasted. The witness knows of but one instance of the taking of cattle
belonging to Defendant in which instance notes were taken separately for the
cattle of Defendant. If the Defendant were to employ an agent, it would depend
upon the honesty of that person whether he were dealt with fairly. The property
of the Defendant consists chiefly of cattle and a few horses to mind them with.*

If a person were to tell him that he owned but one half of the present number of his cattle, he would not know better. This Defendant has a just idea of the number of cattle and other property which he owns. If he was informed that he had but half the number, he would probably distrust it and institute inquiry into the fact.

Whether he would inquire would depend on the person who gave the information. [Defendant] *never rides out to his vacharie* [ranch] *which is about three miles off. The witness knows persons who are large cattle holders and who do not visit their vacheries more than once a year and then see but a small part of them. Vacherie owners are in almost all instances dependant upon the honesty of their stock keepers. Commonly stock holders visit their vacheries occasionally. The defendant does not move about much. He goes to see his children sometimes. He cannot go without assistance. In narration the Defendant frequently repeats the same fact several times, which the witness thinks proceeds from weakness of mind. He sometimes forgets in half an hour what he has said and repeats it again. This is not always the case but sometimes happens. The witness does not recollect things himself as well. The witness does not think he could be easily cheated himself. He thinks the Defendant is in his dotage.* [Yet] *he talks rationally about his affairs.*

Hardy Coward

George McDougal, witness for Defendant, Sworn Testimony. I have known the Defendant for the past 16 or 15 years and during several years of that time lived within a half mile of his residence. For the last five or less years he has had an opportunity of knowing how he [Defendant] *managed his affairs. He has been in the habit of frequent conversations with Defendant on the subject of his affairs. He seems to understand his condition and that they are under his control as far as witness can judge. He never heard the Defendant complain that it was otherwise. The property of the Defendant consists chiefly of cattle and a few horses. He does not know that the cattle of the Defendant have been managed infrequently or improperly. He does not know that any of his property or cattle have been wasted or improperly used. He never heard the Defendant complain of anything of the kind. From conversations had with this Defendant, he thinks he has as much knowledge of his affairs as any man of his age. The Defendant speaks as rationally about his own affairs as about the ordinary concerns of life as most persons. The witness has been present at the branding of some of the cattle of Defendant, and the same precautions were used that usually are. He has heard the Defendant giving directions to Jordan Perkins to sell the cattle that were fit for market since the institution of this suit. He observed it was necessary in consequence of the suit to give these instructions in presence of witnesses. When the Defendant heard of the institution of the suit, he complained that his children wished to deprive him of his property, which he*

*had earned by his own labor. And that he could live with none of his children
except Jordan Perkins in consequence of this complaint and unkind treatment.
The Defendant stated that Jordan Perkins, alone of all his children, treated him
kindly. He has been living at Jordan Perkins's for the last six years. He went
there before he lost his eyesight. He thinks his eyesight has become very bad for
the last two or three years. The witness does not know that the property of the
Defendant has or has not diminished during that time from waste or otherwise.
He believes the cattle of the Defendant to be as much under his control as of
most cattle holders. John Ivey has a vacherie in witness's neighborhood which he
has not seen but once for six years.*

X His mark
George McDougal

*Hardy Coward was called again. When witness says that the Defendant is
not infirm, he means to say that he is not more so than [other] persons of his
age. Persons of his age are generally infirm. His blindness considered, he is more
infirm than [other] persons of his age. When he says that Defendant speaks
reasonably, he means as far as [or depends upon] the information he gets in
relation to his business. He does not know that information is withheld from
him in relation to his business. The witness states that he saw a horse of Joshua
Perkins's lost on a horse race by his stock keeper in December last. He does not
know that property of the Defendant has been wasted or lost since his blindness.
The Defendant has stated to witness that his intentions [are] to leave all his
cattle equally divided among his children. He never heard the Defendant say [he
was] unable to attend to his business.*

Hardy Coward

*George McDougal was called again. He says that the Defendant moves about
the premises of his son, Joshua* [He probably means Jordan.] *Perkins unassisted
and goes to his meals alone. The Defendant was in the town of Opelousas at the
November time of the Court for 1836. He came in on horseback.*

X His mark
George X McDougal

*Burrel Eaves for Defendant was sworn. He says he has known the Defendant,
Joshua Perkins, since April 1836. He believes him to be of perfectly sound mind
but is blind. He believes that he is perfectly competent to manage his own contracts and does not think he could be cheated. He thinks the Defendant has a
perfect knowledge of the state of his affairs and of the manner in which they are
conducted. He knows of* [many dollars?] *that pass out or come in. He lives fifteen miles from the Defendant and has been in the habit of seeing him frequent-*

ly since he has resided in that neighborhood. The Defendant's cattle and stock graze in the immediate vicinity of witness. He does not know whether they increase or not. He has been in the habit of frequently consulting with the Defendant on the state of his affairs, finds him to speak perfectly sensibly in relation to them and seems to understand them as well as witness does his own affairs. Cross-Examination: Defendant is very old, complains of old age and is blind. He is a very stout man for his age. He moves about with the end of a stick. He goes to an outhouse, to the dinner table and takes the same seat without assistance. He only knows that the Defendant knows of the incoming and outgoing of his money from his own representations. He seems always very keen in making contracts for the sale of his holdings. He does not know whether his memory [the Defendant] *is impaired. He has always found him to recollect all orders and requests made to witness for medicines even after the lapse of six weeks or more. Whenever the witness has wished to trade with his sons for the cattle of the Defendant, they have always sent him to the old man* [Defendant] *whom witness has found too hard and close to deal with. He has no knowledge that any of the Defendant's. property is wasted with his not being consulted. Sworn to & Subscribed at Opelousas this 4th day of December A.D. 1837 Before same, Burral Eaves.*

Garrett M. Wilborn for the Defendant was sworn. He says he has known the Defendant since 1831. His mind is as good now as it was when he first knew him. He has heard Burrel Eaves testimony and confirms his statements in every respect. The witness lives about 12 miles from Defendant Sworn to and Subscribed at Opelousas this 4th day of December AD 1837 by G M Wilborn

Ashworth & Perkins	Probate Court
Versus	No. 149
Perkins	Parish of St. Landry

Testimony of Jim Allain [possibly Allen or Allin] *and Aaron Drake taken by consent, subject to all legal exceptions. Aaron Drake, being asked whether he was not allied to the plaintiffs in the above entitled, states that he is the son-in-law of Jesse Ashworth, one of the plaintiffs.* [The] *witness was objected to on the part of Defendant's counsel on the grounds of incompetency. The witness stated that Joshua Perkins, the defendant, is blind. He stated that Defendant told him that he wished to divide his property among his children. He wished this to be done before he died.* [He said] *that it* [the property] *was being destroyed. He stated that he does not believe the Defendant is capable of managing his concerns on account of blindness. He is very feeble but is not bodily afflicted, and he does not think the defendant could manage his business if he were not blind. In conversing with him upon any subject, he moves frequently in a few minutes after the conversation and asks the individual with whom he had been conversing what he said. He would frequently ask questions that had a short time before been asked by him and answered. Witness states that he does not think the Defendant is of sound mind. He would forget circumstances that have been related to him in the course of two hours or half a day. Any person might cheat the Defendant very easily. He states that he does not know how well the Defendant is. The witness when asked why Defendant has not divided his property says that he does not know, unless it is on account of Jordan Perkins. When he [the Defendant] is in Jordan Perkins's presence he speaks as if he were opposed to a division of his property and when out of his presence, the reverse. The Defendant some time past spoke a good deal relative to his property. The defendant does not recollect of what his property consists. The defendant knows that he has property but not how much. His property is much wasted. The Defendant does [not] know how much property he has, nor does witness know that any body else knows. The Defendant says that his property is wasting, but that [he] could not attend to it. The witness heard the defendant say about two years ago that he wanted his property divided among his children in presence of Wilson Carson [?] and others. He does not recollect who the other persons were. He [the defendant] lives at the house of his son, Jordan Perkins. The Defendant forgets what he is told him about his property being destroyed. The last conversation witness had with Defendant was in July last. He then recollected that his property was being wasted and destroyed. He does not know that any person had told him a short time before whether his property was being wasted. The Defendant forgets most any conversation but witness cannot refer to any particular cases.*

Jim Allain, being sworn, states that about twenty months ago the Defendant was coming into Opelousas and stopped at his house. The Defendant observed to witness [that] he did not know him. He was blind. But hearing him speak, he says that he knows him well. [The witness] says that the defendant got down from his horse, and the witness took him by the hand to lead him into the house. The Defendant was shown to a room by witness, since he could not walk into it on account of blindness. The Defendant told him he was sick. After lying in bed in the room for a couple of hours, Deponent told him to come to dinner. The Defendant told he was too sick and fatigued. After lying in bed some time longer, the witness went to his bed and assisted him to the table. He complained of being weak and sick. After Defendant reached the table, he told witness he could not see at all. Defendant told deponent that he could not manage or attend to his business at all, witness says. His wife was compelled to feed defendant with a spoon when the cutter [?] was at his house at the time aforementioned, Witness says. The defendant would some times talk continually,

but he would frequently when speaking of one subject, talk of others matters that had no connection with the first. Witness asked defendant how he attended to his business and the cutter [?] *replied that he could not attend to it. Says that he could attend to his business only by feeling on account of blindness. That defendant told him Jordan Perkins managed his affairs.*
Filed 20 August 1838

August 31st 1838, Notarized in St. Landry Parish, Jim Allain
X his mark
Aaron Drake
Robert Taylor, Clerk[13]

On August 7, 1840, the case was dropped from the Court of Probate upon the request of James Ashworth.[14] At least one researcher believes the case was dismissed because Joshua Perkins had died.[15] However, there are no records of a death and burial for Joshua. The important information is found in the testimony itself. Joshua was probably fairly wealthy because he had extensive cattle and land. There certainly was enough property to provoke a family squabble. Although the daughters and their husbands claimed Joshua was unable to manage his affairs, he lived with his son, Jordan. What seems to be at stake here is who would inherit the ailing father's lands and cattle.

Joshua Perkins had served in the Revolutionary War, according to one witness. The tradition among the Perkins and Sweats was that they had fought with General Marion during the war in South Carolina. One witness seems to confirm the fact that Joshua was mustered. Since the court makes clear that the plaintiffs and defendant are free persons of color, their status as this ethnic or racial designation is in conformity with tradition and the census records of the time.

The second case actually occurred prior to this one. The cases are placed out of sequence because that was the order in which they were discovered. As noted earlier, this was also a case of an interfamily squabble.

In 1829, Delaney Taylor, wife of John Bass, filed suit against Gilbert Swett or Sweat in St. Landry Parish.[16] Mrs. Bass was seeking part of the

---

[13]*Mary Perkins et al. vs. Joshua Perkins*, 149 Court of Probate, 1837.

[14]*Mary Perkins et al. vs. Joshua Perkins*, Court of Probate St. Landry no. 149, 25 August 1840.

[15]Erbon Wise, unpublished account (1983).

[16]*Delaney Taylor wife of John Bass versus Gilbert Swett*, St. Landry Parish District

property owned by Swett/Sweat in the wake of her mother's death. Gilbert Swett apparently ran away with Frances Smith in 1777. She at that time was legally married to John Barney Taylor. It is unclear whether Gilbert Swett and Frances Smith ever married. Delaney Taylor and John Bass were attempting to establish a marriage between Swett and Smith, and therefore a basis for inheritance on the part of Delaney Taylor. Testifying for the plaintiff were James Groves and Aaron Dial, among others. Gilbert Swett on May 19, 1830 petitioned for a deposition to be taken from "Joshua Perkins f.m.c. [free man of color]—residing near the Sabine River in the Parish of St. Landry" Following is the transcribed text of that deposition.

[Joshua Perkins's Testimony]

"*Joshua Perkins, f.m.c.* [free man of color], *being duly sworn to testify in the aforesaid case under the order aforesaid—Saith—He is seventy-one years old in November next and was born on Little Pedee* [now Pee Dee] *River in the present state of South Carolina in what is now, he is informed, called the Marion District. He has known John Bass and Delaney Taylor, his wife, the Plaintiffs, from childhood. He has sometimes has not seen them for several years at a time. He has known the Defendant ever since he was a boy. Sometimes they were separated for several years,* [but] *then they came together again. The Defendant was born in South Carolina on the Pedee River, near the place where the Witness was born. He was in his lifetime acquainted with Frances Smith, deceased. He first became acquainted with her about the year 1777 in South Carolina in the same part of the country where he lived. He thinks he never saw said Frances Smith, deceased, until after she went off with the Defendant. He never saw John Barney Taylor but once that he can recollect and that was when he went with the Defendant to carry off the aforesaid Frances Smith, deceased. It was in the year 1777 he believes—in the same part of the country where he was born—fourteen or fifteen miles distant. He always understood that the aforesaid Frances Smith, deceased, was the wife of John Barney Taylor. They always passed in that part of the country as man and wife. When Defendant went off with her, she was spoken of as John Barney Taylor's wife. It was in the year 1777 that the Witness went with the Defendant to assist him in carrying off the aforesaid Frances Smith, deceased. When they went to the house where she was, they found a man there who the Witness was told was John Barney Taylor, the husband of said Frances Smith, deceased. The witness lent the Defendant a horse to carry off the aforesaid Frances Smith, deceased. When the Witness and Defendant first went to the house and found Taylor there, they*

Court, case 1533, 27 August 1829.

went off and afterwards got the aforesaid Frances Smith, deceased, out, and she went off with the Defendant. At the time the aforesaid Frances Smith, deceased, went off with the Defendant, John Barney Taylor was alive. He never saw him [again]. *He never heard he was dead. He is an old acquaintance of the Defendant. He has known him from boyhood. He has sometimes lived near him and has been for several years without even seeing him. He is always friendly with Defendant. He never knew of the marriage of the aforesaid Frances Smith, deceased, with the Defendant. He thinks from the intimacy that has always existed between them* [Swett and Smith], *that if there had ever been any marriage, he should have known of it. He has lived near Defendant in South Carolina, North Carolina, & Tennessee. He came with Defendant when he left Tennessee and came on to Big Black River in Mississippi. He lived near him there and removed to Opelousas about the same time that the Defendant did. He has seen him frequently since he lived in Opelousas and been at his house. He arrived in Louisiana about twenty-six years past. He never knew or heard of the death of John Barney Taylor. He has heard it spoken of that the Defendant and said Frances Smith, deceased, were not married. He always believed so himself and believes that such was the impression with all those who knew them well and for a long time. He is no relation to the Defendant. The Defendant is, he believes, about seventy three or four years of age.*

Cross examination by Plaintiffs Counsel.
He thinks he heard that John Barney Taylor went off with the Army about fifty-three years ago. He never saw him [again]. *He thinks he heard that said Taylor was killed or died in the Army, but he is not sure. The witness was then about seventeen years old. He heard it said that Defendant and Frances Smith, deceased, had afterwards got married but he was not present himself.*
Examined by Defendant Counsel. He says that he has heard that one Trouble-field married them. He does not know that said Troublefield had any authority to marry any person. He said Troublefield was not as the Witness thinks a Justice of the Peace or Judge but was a sort of a preacher he believes.
Joshua Perkins, X His mark
Sworn and subscribed
To by making his ordinary mark
At Opelousas in the Parish of St.
Landry this 25th day of May in the
Year 1830 before me

Henderson Taylor Justice of the Peace
Acting in the
Parish of St. Landry

The foregoing testimony is to be read in the trial of the case of John Bass &
Wife vs. Gilbert Sweat, No. 1533 in the District Court of St. Landry, subject
to all legal exceptions
Except as to the time, place and manner of taking the same. Opelousas May
25th, 1830

Thos. H. Serris pffs. Atty.
R. Garland Atty.
For Defendant (District court No. 1533, 1830)

Like the prior legal proceedings, this testimony provides some important factual evidence to add to this story. According to the order to obtain testimony, Joshua Perkins was living on the Louisiana side of the Sabine River in 1830. This area is part of the Neutral Zone or "No-Man's-Land" that lay between the Calcasieu and Sabine Rivers. Although considered a place of lawlessness, the courts of Louisiana provided government for the people in this area. In addition Joshua may have lived there for the next several years. That would lend credibility to his son herding cattle back and forth across the Texas-Louisiana border and to Washington Perkins account of being born in Calcasieu Parish.

Joshua, by his own testimony, lived near Gilbert Swett in the states of South Carolina, North Carolina, Tennessee, Mississippi, and Louisiana. He provides a migration pattern that can be traced through census records and land deeds. Where Joshua was not listed, Gilbert provided additional evidence of location. Earlier in the total transcript, testimony states that Gilbert Swett came to Louisiana twenty-four to twenty-five years prior to the filing of the case in 1829. That would mean that he arrived about 1804 or 1805. Since Joshua presumably traveled with Gilbert, he would have arrived at the same time.

Joshua Perkins stated that he was born near Gilbert Swett. Gilbert is presumed to have been born in North Carolina around 1758 and was listed in the 1790 Census of North Carolina in Morgan District, Burke County. Joshua Perkins is listed in the same census.[17] This information is helpful in verifying Joshua's birthplace and potentially his parents. Even though he stated that he was born on the Little Pee Dee River in South Carolina, there is evidence that the border between these states changed. The Yadkin/Pee

---

[17] Erbon W. Wise, *Sweat Families of the South* (Sulphur LA: E. W. Wise, 1983) 11. U.S. Bureau of the Census, Heads of Families-North Carolina, 1790, 107.

Dee River and Lumber River of North Carolina merge in South Carolina to become the Little Pee Dee and then Great Pee Dee.

Based on the date of the testimony and Joshua's reported age, we have information concerning his year of birth. The testimony was taken in May 1830. Joshua testified that he would be seventy-one years of age in November of 1830. His year of birth thus appears to be 1759. This information, provided by him in testimony, creates the opportunity to distinguish him from others who might have the same name.

Finally, Joshua is listed in the court transcripts as "f.m.c." This designation mirrors the census determination that Joshua Perkins was a "free man of color." It also matches the court records for the later trial involving his children. Despite the use of the term f.m.c. or free man of color, it was still not clear what was the source of the ethnic origins of this man and his family.

The censuses of Louisiana and Texas had been searched. Now it was time to go backwards to the states where Joshua and his friends had come from. The courts would provide answers again. But first it was necessary to take a closer look at Reverend Joseph Willis.

Were you born of wind and sun?
This bright shining spirit who stood so tall.

Did you know your mother?
Did you spend your youth as your father's slave

Without the love and nurture of a mother's touch?
You outlived four wives and led them all

Halfway across the continent
Where your dark skin found souls to save.

They say that labels never counted
Your dreams were always there.

They say the greatness of your journey
Is all that we remember for today?

Hundreds of descendants, members,
Families were nurtured by your care.

The passion of your mission
Paved the others' way.

Chapter 5

The Apostle to the Opelousas

One of the most astounding stories uncovered in our research is that of the Reverend Joseph Willis. According to the accounts of historians and relatives and his own personal story, Joseph Willis was born in the late 1700s in North Carolina to Agerton Willis, a British colonist, and Agerton's female slave. One source states that Joseph was born in 1764.[1] Another source stated that Willis was born in 1759, the same year as Joshua Perkins.[2] Willis himself told his children that he had been born a slave to Agerton Willis and that his mother was one-half Cherokee Indian.

According to one family source, Agerton Willis attempted to free his son Joseph via a will written and signed on September 18, 1776.[3] At the time of Agerton's death, accounts indicate that Agerton's eldest brother, Daniel, wrote to Governor Caswell objecting to the terms of the will and the fact that Joseph was not only a slave but not of age to inherit his father's property. (Depending on his actual birth date, Joseph would have been between twelve and seventeen years old.) Eleven years later, Joseph's cousin, John Willis, a member of the North Carolina legislature, passed a law giving Joseph his freedom. The following is the text of this act.

---

[1]U.S. Bureau of the Census, Heads of Families-North Carolina, 1790, 125.

[2]Leon Terrell, *The History of Calvary Baptist Church at Bayou Chicot* (Ville Platt LA: L. Terrell, 1992) 6.

[3]Randy (Randall Lee) Willis, "Joseph Willis: The First Baptist Preacher of the Word West of the Mississippi River," unpublished manuscript (1998). Now published online as "Joseph Willis, the Apostle to the Opelousas, the First Baptist Preacher of the Gospel of Jesus Christ West of the Mississippi River," <http://www.randywillis.org/joseph.html> (c2000).

CHAPTER XXXV.

An Act to Emancipate Certain Persons therein mentioned.

Whereas Agerton Willis, late of Bladen county, was in his lifetime possessed of a certain slave called Joseph, and in consideration of the services of him the said Joseph, and the particular obligations he conceived himself under to the said Joseph for his fidelity and attention, did by his last will and testament devise to the said Joseph his freedom and emancipation, and did also give unto the said Joseph a considerable property, both real and personal: And whereas the executor and next of kin to the said Joseph did in pursuance of the said will take counsel thereon, and were well advised that the same could not by any means take effect, but would be of prejudice to the said slave and subject him still as property of the said Agerton Willis; whereupon the said executor and next of kin, together with the heirs of the said Agerton Willis, deceased, did cause a fair and equal distribution of the said estate, as well to do equity and justice in the said case of Joseph, as in pursuance of their natural love and affection to the said Agerton, and did resolve on the freedom of the said Joseph and to give an equal proportion of the said estate: Wherefore,

I. Be it Enacted by the General Assembly of the State of North Carolina, and it is hereby Enacted by the authority of the same, That from and after the passing of this Act, the said Joseph shall and is hereby declared to be emancipated and set free; and from henceforward he be called and known by the name of Joseph Willis, by which name he may take, hold, occupy, possess and enjoy to him and his heirs forever, all and singular the property both real and personal so given him by the said distribution of the said executors, heirs and next of kin, and by the said name of Joseph Willis shall henceforward be entitled to all the rights and privileges of a free person of mixed blood: Provided nevertheless, That this act shall not extend to enable the said Joseph by himself or attorney, or any other person in trust for him, in any manner to commence or prosecute any suit or suits for any other property but such as may be given him by this act or such as he may have acquired by his own industry, but this act may in all such cases be plead in bar, and the property therein given be considered as a full and ample consideration for the final accommodation and settlement of all doubts concerning the freedom and property either real, personal or mixed belonging or in any manner appertaining to the said Joseph.[4]

---

[4]Walter Clark, coll. and ed. "An Act to Emancipate Certain Persons therein mentioned," *The State Records of North Carolina: Laws 1797–1788* (Goldsboro NC:

While most of Willis's descendants will agree that the documentation shows he was born a slave, the nature of his race will ever be disputed. Daniel Willis made reference to Joseph as a "Molata" [*sic*] boy in his letter to Governor Caswell disputing Willis's right to his father's land.[5] However, the descendants would claim that any mixed race person in North Carolina, whether Indian or African, was called mulatto, family members would recount a story that claimed Joseph Willis's mother was a Cherokee Indian or half Cherokee and half white.

At some point in this history, Joseph Willis is purported to have been in South Carolina, where, like the Perkins men, he claimed to have fought with General Francis Marion, the "Swamp Fox." Marion spent much of his time recruiting a ragtag group of soldiers along the Pee Dee River. They were described as "some white, some black, and all mounted."[6]

By 1790 residents living just south of the North Carolina border included a Joshua and Isaac Perkins and Joseph Willis.[7] Descendants of Joseph stated that he told his grandchildren that after receiving his inheritance, he "left North Carolina with nothing but a horse, bridle, saddle, and the money from the sale of his property."[8] Family historians record his first marriage to Rachel Brafford during this period.[9] Children from the first marriage included Agerton, named for Willis's father. A second wife, Sarah, followed the death of Rachel.

Between 1791 and 1804, a number of men were ordained and licensed by the head of Enoree Church in South Carolina. This church was one of the earliest Baptist churches under the Bethel Association in Greenville County, South Carolina. Among the ordained and licensed ministers was

---

Nash Brothers, 1905) 929-30. Randy Willis quotes relevant parts of this act in his essay on "Joseph Willis."

[5]Walter Clark, coll. and ed. "Daniel Willis Senr. to Gov. Caswell Respecting Admtn. &C," *The State Records of North Carolina*, vol. 11, 1776 (Winston-Salem NC: M. I. & J. C. Stewart Printers, 1895) 780.

[6]Benson J. Lossing, *The Pictorial Field-Book of the Revolution*, vol. 2 (Rutland VT: Charles E. Tuttle Co., 1972) 479.

[7]U.S. Bureau of the Census, Heads of Families—South Carolina, Cheraw District, 1790, 49.

[8]Randy Willis, "Joseph Willis: First Baptist Preacher of the Word West of the Mississippi River," 6.

[9]Wise, *Sweat Families of the South*, 126.

Joseph Willis.[10] Willis, along with two other ministers, petitioned to have the congregation incorporated in 1799.

During his time in South Carolina, Joseph Willis became friends with Richard Curtis, Jr. Curtis became involved in establishing churches farther west and was the first pastor of Salem Baptist Church in Amite County, Mississippi.[11] In the later 1700s Willis traveled to Mississippi with Richard Curtis. He was recorded as one of three ministers (with William Thompson and Richard Curtis) that helped organize the "Baptist Church on Buffaloe [Creek]" in October 1798.[12] According to family lore, Willis went back to South Carolina to get his family. He moved to Mississippi with the other associated families in the late 1700s to early 1800s.

Another version of the same story recounts a discovery by Richard Curtis that many of the people he needed to minister to were Indians. Mississippi was the home of the Choctaw Nation. Curtis remembered his good friend Joseph Willis, who was part Indian. He believed Willis would be an acceptable missionary to the Indian nation so he went to South Carolina to persuade Willis to visit Mississippi. Willis was impressed with the possibilities in Mississippi so he returned to South Carolina and gathered his possessions and family and collected his friends. They made the trip together across Tennessee and down the Natchez Trace to a place along the Mississippi River.

All accounts agree that in the early 1800s, the group crossed the river and entered into Louisiana. Willis would travel to the town of Bayou Chicot, where he preached his first sermon. He became the first Baptist minister to preach west of the Mississippi. Here he established the Calvary Baptist Church in 1804, which still stands today. He also would marry a third time, after the death of his second wife. His third wife was probably Martha or Mary Johnson, most likely a member of one of the other families who traveled west with Willis.

From this marriage were born a number of children, including Martha Willis in 1825. Three daughters were born prior to Martha, and their names are unrecorded in any public records. It is believed that one of those

---

[10]Leah Townsend, *South Carolina Baptists: 1670–1805* (Baltimore: Clearfield Publishing, 1935) 214.

[11]Glen Lee Greene, *House upon a Rock: About Southern Baptists in Louisiana* (Alexandria: Louisiana Baptist Convention, 1973) 45.

[12]Terrell, *The History of Calvary Baptist Church*, 7.

daughters was Lucinda. She was born around 1824 or 1825, possibly a twin to Martha. In each succeeding generation, there is a Lucinda among the Willis offspring. In the Perkins family, there is a tradition of naming the oldest daughter after the mother's mother. My great-grandmother is named Martha Mary. Also the oral tradition from Rev. Howard Bundick indicates that Lucinda Perkins's maiden name was Willis. There is no other Lucinda Willis for this generation. This Lucinda fits into the timeline of the unnamed Willis daughters. The Perkins family had migrated westward with Joseph Willis, and these families tended to intermarry for generations.

One early Baptist historian wrote that Joseph Willis faced great hardships in coming into Louisiana.[13] According to Paxton, Willis was a "mulatto" and a Baptist arriving in Catholic Louisiana just after the turn of the century. His color was less of a problem in Louisiana because he chose to work in the "Neutral Zone" where "free persons of color" were the rule. However, Willis did have difficulty being approved by the Mississippi Baptist Association to conduct his ministry. The Mississippi Baptists were the oversight group for Louisiana. It took several requests before this body would finally sanction Willis and his ministry. His energy and sense of mission probably enhanced the acceptance of Willis by the Association. Willis would form at least ten churches during his lifetime and foster the religious and spiritual well-being of hundreds of God's children.

Willis lived until 1854 and was buried in the cemetery of Occupy Baptist Church—one of the congregations he started. A tribute to him reads as follows.

> The gospel was proclaimed by him in these regions before the American flag was hoisted here. Before the church began to send out missionaries into destitute regions, he, at his own expense, and frequently at the risk of his life, came to these parts preaching the gospel of the Redeemer. For fifty years he was instant in season and out of season, preaching, exhorting and instructing; regarding not his property, his health, or even his life, if he might be the means of turning sinners to Christ.[14]

The debate over Willis's origins persists even into modern times. In the 1930s, one of his descendants, Greene Wallace Strother, wrote his Master

---

[13]W. E. Paxton, *A History of the Baptists of Louisiana from the Earliest Times to the Present* (St. Louis: Barnes, 1888) 15.
[14]Paxton, *A History of the Baptists of Louisiana.*

of Theology thesis to prove that Joseph Willis had no "Negro" blood.[15] In the introduction, the author sets out "to present a clear argument that would establish the fact that Joseph Willis's father was an Englishman and his mother part Indian and all the other blood in his veins was Anglo-Saxon."[16] The author goes on to say that he does not intend to "reflect upon any other race." Yet he explains that he has named his son, Joseph Willis, and he wants his son to know that his name is honorable. The implication, of course, is that to be of mixed race is dishonorable.

The author begins by relating a series of facts, specifically Joseph Willis's origins. In order to place this argument into context, "fact" number seven is transcribed verbatim:

> That the racial connections of the people among whom he [Willis] lived in later life was called in question and he made affidavit before John Philipps of Glenmore, La., that his father was an Englishman and his mother was part Indian, and there was not a drop of Negro blood in his veins. This affidavit was on file in the courthouse at Alexandria, La., but due to the courthouse being destroyed by fire during the Civil War, this affidavit was lost.[17]

Strother substantiates these "facts" through the specific stories and statements of various family members. He adds a fourth point of proof by stating that "no direct descendant of Joseph Willis ever had anything other than the features and hair of an Anglo-Saxon or Indian, and whatever of brunette complexion, it was naturally the hue of the Indian." This "evidence" along with the missing affidavit became for the next sixty years the primary arguments against the possibility of any African heritage. It is noteworthy that the reason Willis made his affidavit was because of "the racial connections of the people among which he lived." Census records show that Willis lived among other Red Bone families with the names of Perkins, Goins, Ashworths, Bunch, and Dial.

Strother begins the second chapter of his thesis, "The Error," with quotations from David Benedict's discussion of Baptist history.[18] According to

---

[15]Greene W. Strother, "About Joseph Willis" (Th.M. thesis, Baptist Bible Institute, New Orleans, 1934) 2.

[16]Strother, "About Joseph Willis," 2.

[17]Strother, "About Joseph Willis."

[18]Strother quotes the classic David Benedict, *A General History of the Baptist Denomination in America and Other Parts of the World*, 1-vol. ed. (New York: Lewis Colby and Co., 1848).

Strother, Benedict referred to Joseph Willis as a mulatto. He also stated that others had positive stories to tell about "the ministerial labors and distinguished usefulness of the aged *colored* minister."[19] Strother states that the testimony of descendants denies this racial designation given to Willis.

Much of Strother's thesis consists of letters from people, some of whom did not know Willis directly. For example, a 1894 letter to the author's relative, J. H. Strother, stated that Willis "was not a mulatto, but was somewhat mixed, and very dark skin [*sic*]." The letter was signed by John O'Quin who later told the author that "his descendants knew that Joseph Willis was not mixed Negro blood."[20] Strother points out that John O'Quin said that Willis "was 'somewhat mixed,' but 'mixed' with what, he never says."[21] However, Strother goes on to talk about the rumors, which placed "a reproach" against his name and that of his descendants.[22]

One letter from J. H. Strother to Greene Strother implies that living among some of the early settlers with unsavory backgrounds "put our ancestors in their embarrassing position."[23] However, many of the names identified are the same as the names of those families who migrated with Rev. Joseph Willis to Louisiana. J. H. Strother later professes to believe that the "old men from the Carolinas, except 'Father Willis' were Croatans."[24] This comment is very interesting because of the Croatan theory related to another mixed-race group, the Melungeons. According to Greene Strother, J. H. Strother actually says that Willis's third wife, a Miss Johnson, was one of the Carolina group.[25]

The issue of Rev. Willis's racial makeup became so important that in 1930, his son, Aimuwell Willis, signed a sworn affidavit in Vernon Parish that his father was not a mulatto. In this same statement Aimuwell confirms that his paternal grandfather was an Englishman and that his grandmother was part Indian. The reason for this affidavit appeared to be an effort to remove Rev. Willis's name from the *Negro Year Book*. According to Greene Strother, Willis had been listed in the 1921–1922 edition of the year book

---

[19]Strother, "About Joseph Willis," 5-6; emphasis added.
[20]Strother, "About Joseph Willis," 9.
[21]Strother, "About Joseph Willis," 11.
[22]Strother, "About Joseph Willis," 12.
[23]Strother, "About Joseph Willis," 23.
[24]Strother, "About Joseph Willis," 34.
[25]Strother, "About Joseph Willis," 24.

on page 200,[26] and Willis was also profiled in the *History of Louisiana Negro Baptists . . . 1804–1914.*[27] The paragraph in the yearbook contains all the other details told about Willis, except for the racial designation.

The sole purpose of Greene Strother's master's thesis was to prove that Joseph Willis had no Negro blood. But were the reports of the various descendants and the effort to remove his name from the *Negro Year Book* the end of the speculation? A history of Louisiana Baptists published in 1973 made no reference to Rev. Joseph Willis's racial makeup in the body of the text. However, in appendix A, the author writes a two-page account devoted entirely to Joseph Willis. He again quotes the Paxton description of Willis as mulatto. The author posits that Paxton wrote this in his history because "Willis's closest friends and associates, who loved and respected him, believed that he was mulatto or that he was at least part Negro."[28] In his master's thesis, Glen Greene repeats some of the statements made by Greene Strother. He also makes reference to the "unusual ethnic strain" of Willis's third wife and that his fourth wife was "of an ethnic group of uncertain origin," specifically Red Bone.[29] Willis's fourth wife was Elvie Sweat, of the Swett/Sweat family who had accompanied Willis to Louisiana.

Glen Greene states that "Even it were of vital importance, it seems now impossible to determine the precise ethnic background of Joseph Willis."[30] He believes Willis may have been simply part Indian and recognizes that most Americans cannot give an adequate ethnic description of their background. Willis's descendants included many dedicated men and women devoted to the religious profession. And although there would also be a fair share of scoundrels, the proportion of the family that were of any particular profession and social standing most likely was varied. The traits that constituted the rest of my family would bear this out.

---

[26]Strother, "About Joseph Willis," 66. Strother refers to Monroe Nathan Work, *Negro Year Book: An Annual Encyclopedia of the Negro, 1921–1922*, 6th ed. (Tuskegee AL: Negro Year Book Pub. Co., 1922).

[27]William Hicks, *History of Louisiana Negro Baptists and Early Beginnings, from 1804 to 1914*, ed. Sue L. Eakin, repr. with new material (Lafayette: University of Southwestern Louisiana, 1915; original: Nashville: National Baptist Pub. Board, 1914) 251.

[28]Greene, *House upon a Rock*, 325.

[29]Greene, *House upon a Rock*, 326.

[30]Greene, *House upon a Rock*, 326.

Despite attempts to "whiten" Joseph Willis's background, it is interesting to note that he is described with great pride as an early black Baptist pioneer as well. The following is quoted from a recently published book by a black Baptist historian.

> Again, with certain patterns now well established, the independent or separate Black church movement extended southward to Louisiana. The extension of Baptist faith and practice to this region was connected with the great frontier movement of the Protestant church. During the colonial period, the primary religious work in this area was carried on by the Roman Catholic Church. However, with the coming of Joseph Willis (1762–1864) a *free black* from South Carolina, a new religious dimension was introduced to the territory of Louisiana prior to its political ties with the United States. Willis initially migrated to Mississippi with other migrants in 1798. From the southwestern part of that territory Joseph Willis went forth as an apostle to the Opelousa Indians in the year of 1804. The territory of this Indian nation was Louisiana at Bayou Chicot.[31]

So Rev. Joseph Willis is identified as both a white and black religious pioneer.

Some of Willis's direct descendants have been working on an account of his life, reaching back to Joseph Willis's father, Agerton, and Agerton's brothers. The stories of Rev. Joseph Willis have been available on websites, through e-mail listservs, and genealogical association newsletters.[32]

A few years ago John Locklear posted an exception to the stories of Willis's racial background as only Indian and white. The following is part of one posting.

> The Willis[es] once lived close to my ancestors near the Saddletree Swamp in Robeson County (North Carolina). I am aware of the fact that there were some Indian Slaves in Colonial America, but there were not any in the Robeson County area of North Carolina. Some early Indians in Robeson County owned land, and even fewer owned slaves, but it is apparent that these slaves were of African origin. During that period of time all of our

---

[31]Leroy Fitts, *A History of Black Baptists* (Nashville: Broadman Press, 1985) 48-49; emphasis added.

[32]See, e.g., Randy (Randall Lee) Willis, "Joseph Willis: The Apostle to the Opelousas. The First Baptist Preacher of the Gospel of Jesus Christ West of the Mississippi River," online at <http://www.randywillis.org/joseph.html>. This website also has links to a number of subsites.

people, the Indians here in Robeson County, did have surnames. And no, we did not enjoy all of the rights of our white counterparts, but we were by law classified as "Free People of Color," and enslaved by no man. I believe yours is a story that align [*sic*] closer to that of Thomas Jefferson and Sally Hemmingway [*sic*]. Your ancestor Joseph Willis, was born a slave and had to be emancipated from slavery. In Robeson County, North Carolina our Indian ancestors never found the need to be emancipated, because we were born and lived free.[33]

It should be noted at this point that the name Locklear is very common among the Lumbee Indians of North Carolina.[34] Like Red Bones, the Lumbee Indians are considered by genealogical historians to be triracial isolates. However, another group classifies them as Melungeons, the mysterious mixed-race people especially of Tennessee and North Carolina. For the purposes of this discussion, Locklear was attempting to get specific facts: "I will be glad to receive that documentation," he said, "and change my views on the subject should you be able to substantiate the claim."[35]

Locklear's most pertinent point was that Native Americans were not slaves in North Carolina. Mr. Locklear claims to be descended from a mixed-Indian group. He admitted that Indian slavery was practiced in other states, but had no evidence of the same being practiced in North Carolina. According to Locklear, he has thoroughly researched his ancestors and the issues around their racial origins.

Some Willis descendents argue that the information about Joseph Willis's origins is correct, and base their defense on the following points. Agerton Willis is shown to have a household of himself and five male slaves. There is no mention of female slaves, so his descendant presumes that Rev. Willis's mother died soon after his birth.

Second, the descendant states that "Rev. Willis testified for over seventy years that his mother was part-Cherokee Indian and his father was English. In fact, to be exact, he said his mother was half-Cherokee Indian." This argument rests with the "lost" deposition given by Joseph Willis before his death. While the affidavit itself was "destroyed in a fire," members of the family recall stories of such a statement. And they argued that Rev. Willis

---

[33]John Locklear, e-mail correspondence, 2000.
[34]Walton-Raji, *Black Indian Genealogy Research*, 95.
[35]John Locklear, e-mail Correspondence, 2000.

was such a fine, upstanding minister, he would never lie. One chronicler of Rev. Willis goes on to state the following:

> He could not have been part-Black because he legally married three white women in Louisiana and South Carolina in the late 1700s and early 1800s. It was against the law for a mulatto/Negro to do so. Frankly, I wish he had been a Black or part-Black slave; to think a man who was part-Black could establish the first five all-white churches in Louisiana in the very early 1800s would be wonderful. In fact, if that had happened, Joseph Willis would be considered one of the greatest Blacks in history.[36]

It should be noted here that the latter two wives were from what we now believe are Red Bone families and the marriages took place in the Neutral Zone. As to the marriage of white women in Colonial America in the later 1700s, Rev. Willis was not the only mulatto who married white women. It occurred frequently in triracial communities.

The next argument was based on the absence of African features among Willis's descendants. "Note the high cheek bones, beak nose, straight hair, thin lips; hardly Black characteristics."[37] Greene Strother's master's thesis makes similar arguments.[38]

We will never know the full racial makeup of Rev. Willis's mother without DNA testing. Even then the amount of each race may be indeterminate. A recent genetic study of Melungeons has been unable to solve the mystery except to say the modern descendants are a little black, a little Native American, but primarily Eurasian.[39]

The statement that Rev. Willis would be "lying" if he said that he did not have African blood when he did, does not match the experience of other multiracial people. If Rev. Willis's mother died early, he might have been given only partial information about her racial background. Oral tradition in my own family chose to emphasize the Native American heritage. Also any evidence of what Rev. Willis actually knew has been lost.

And as for facial features, my own granddaughter looks Indian or Hispanic. In fact, her father comes from a long line of mixed Native American, African, and English people who were well settled in Maryland

---

[36]Randy Willis, e-mail correspondence, 2000.

[37]Randy Willis, e-mail correspondence, 2000.

[38]Strother, "About Joseph Willis," 44.

[39]Kathleen McGowan, "Where Do We Really Come From?" *Discover* (May 2003): 62.

by the 1790s.[40] Many members of his people do not "look black." However, the family considers themselves African Americans.

A number of family members have repeatedly denied any racial bias, yet strongly denied any possibility of African origins. It is today politically incorrect to demonstrate racial bigotry. However, racism still exists even among those who claim to be the most enlightened.

Denying interracial marriage has its pitfalls also. Most interracial mixing is considered to be the result of white slaveholders taking advantage of the women who were in servitude. However, it is clear from historical accounts that Caucasians and Africans lived in consensual union. The laws that were passed in Colonial America regarding marriage and other unions between white and black couples were in response to this practice.[41] In addition, there was a tradition of "passing" prevalent among light-skinned Negroes.[42]

As for Joseph Willis's mother, the mystery still exists. If she were half-Cherokee and half-white, she would most likely not have been a slave. If she were half-Cherokee and half-black, she had a higher likelihood of being a slave, thus her son would be a slave. The story among the Perkins descendants was that a grandmother had been a Cherokee Indian who had "married" a white man. Could this have been the source of that story?

To confuse matters more, there is the assumption that all tribes in the area were Cherokee. We would discover later that many Native peoples in the Carolinas were immediately classified as Cherokee. We may never know the truth, but the story has become deeply embedded in the family lore, passed from generation to generation. Some people would express shame at having "Indian" blood; however, there was deep pride and curiosity about the Native heritage in Perkins/Smith family members.

While Rev. Joseph Willis would be accepted in his community because of the work he did among the churches of Louisiana, four years after his death the Perkins family would once again face discrimination and disgrace.

---

[40]Extensive records document free Negroes in Maryland and Delaware. Old colonial court cases list the families of Proctor and Savoy, paternal ancestors of my granddaughter. Also Accomack County, Virginia records for the early 1800s show several households of free Negroes with the name of Perkins.

[41]Lawrence R. Tenzer, *A Completely New Look at Interracial Sexuality* (Manahawkin NJ: Scholars Pub. House, 1990).

[42]Charles L. Blockson, *Black Genealogy* (Baltimore: Black Classic Press, 1991) 116-20.

Those family members, who stayed in Tennessee while others migrated to Louisiana, became ensnarled in a famous case based on defamation. The testimony and court trial provides background, which would be used by both sides of the debate about their racial makeup, and that continues to today. And while Rev. Joseph Willis spent his life "saving the souls" of hundreds of hearty Baptists, his friends, the Perkins, were defending themselves against a suggestion, if not a claim, that they were soulless.

The Path of Darkness

In the background, the darkness of racism stands to illuminate the members of this extended clan. We enter the very darkness of the skin of my ancestors and face the pain they faced because they were Other. Even though chapter 6 recounts a trial that occurred more than one hundred years from the birth of Old Jock Perkins, the only known patriarch, the stigma attached to their color makes them deny their heritage. Or were they really unsure about their ancestry? We do not know.

Chapters 6 and 7 were the most painful to write because of the horror of bigotry and the loss of family for the children bound into servitude. These chapters together form the background of whatever data exists for a people known as "Red Bones."[1] We ask the question of the prophet: "How does one learn to recover the darkness and befriend it again."[2]

---

[1](See also esp. chap. 1, n. 1, above.) The origin of the term "Red Bones" is unclear. Most writers who use the term generalize and say that it is a mix of white, Indian, and black. Among genealogists, the term has become synonymous with "triracial." Don C. Marler identifies several theories, including what may be the most reasonable, that it originates with the West Indies term *red-ibo*, pronounced "reddi-bohn" ("Reddy Bone"), which means a *mixture of races*. See Marler's "The Louisiana Redbones" (1997) and his *Redbones of Louisiana* (2003).

[2]Fox, *Original Blessing*, 135.

No soul?
Who are you to decide who has a soul?
No soul?
Who takes the stage to say
that one has a soul or does not have a soul?

What man, in the midst of hatred and bigotry dares to speak?
A speaking?

Taking an oath to whether you are a Negro or not?
Where is the justice in this?

He will take his gun, he says.
He will go down and Kill them, he says.
They are like Mules, he says.
These mulattos when they mix that far have no souls.

Who is this man, filled with evil?
Where does the hatred come from?
Why does he not see the humanity, the spirit, in others?
What grief he must bring then and today through these words?

Chapter 6

In a Tennessee Court

In the mid-1800s, Jacob F. Perkins filed suit against John R. White and others in Knoxville, Tennessee.[1] From the fragments of the court case available, several stories emerge as to the reason for the suit. John White called Perkins a Negro and suggested that he had no right to vote or serve as an election judge.[2] Another historian states that Perkins sued White simply because White called him a "free Negro."[3]

The crux of the case rested on whether the great-grandfather of Jacob was a "Negro" or "Portuguese." Underlying this struggle were the laws that prevented African Americans from enjoying the full rights of other Americans. People of Portuguese descent would be considered "white" Americans whereas those of African descent could not lay claim to legal protections and "privileges" granted to "white" citizens.

In the process of transcribing documents pertaining to the court case, important facts came to light about the family, and about the presence, and lack of, racism, in the mid-1800s. The first important discovery was that Joshua Perkins, the great-grandfather, or "Old Jock" as he was called, came from Pee Dee, South Carolina. This information conformed to the testimony of the Louisiana Joshua Perkins about his birthplace.

In testimony, seventy-seven-year-old Daniel Stout stated that he had known George, Jacob, Joshua, and Lewis for sixty-five years prior to the trial. These men were identified as sons of Old Jock, and Stout reported that they had come from Pee Dee, South Carolina. Thus the lineage of Old Jock as my great-great-great-grandfather is confirmed based on the evidence given in testimony.

---

[1] *Jacob Perkins vs. John White et al.*, 929.2, Thomas A. R. Nelson Papers, Calvin M. McClung Historical Collection, Knox County TN, Library Archives, 1855, 929.

[2] Sandra Loridans, personal correspondence, 1998.

[3] Heinegg, *Free African Americans*, 546.

Catharine Roller, aged eighty, claimed to know the Perkins family as well. She described Old Jock as large, tall, not white but with mixed blood. His wife was fair-skinned and named Mary, according to Ms. Roller. She also knew three of the children: Isaac, Lewis, and Polly. Old Jock's wife, Mary, has been identified as Mary Black by a number of different sources.[4] She was always described as fair-skinned and her ethnic lineage said to be Scottish. Old Jock married Mary (Polly) Black in 1753.

In the chapter on origins, I will explore the conflicting views on Old Jock's ethnicity more thoroughly. This chapter focuses on a historic legal case and on the atmosphere of racism that is delineated in the text of the trial. However, it is important to state the nature of the dispute because it bears on the descriptions to follow.

One set of historians, represented in this case by Professor N. Brent Kennedy, study the group of people called Melungeons who come out of the southern Appalachian Mountains. Melungeons may be triracials, of mixed Indian, white, and Negro ancestry, or simply dark-skinned people of unknown origin.[5] Many of the Melungeon descendants believe their roots are Iberian, Moorish, and Native American.[6] Although they acknowledge that there was intermarriage between Melungeons and Africans, they define Africans as people from the Mediterranean coastal areas, including North Africa, as distinguished from the people from Senegal, Gambia, Angola, and other sites of the slave trade.

Paul Heinegg, Virginia DeMarce, and Gary Mills, all of whom are historians and genealogists, represent another view. Their work points to a mix of the slave-source African countries, Europe, and Native America. The research of DeMarce and Mills deals specifically with the Louisiana Red Bones. However, the Melungeon researchers identify Red Bones as a Melungeon group. Both groups include Old Jock Perkins as a member of their group, even though the Red Bones are the people who departed for Louisiana in the late 1700s to early 1800s. These claims are reminiscent of those related to Rev. Joseph Willis, that is, that Willis was the first *white* Baptist minister *and* the first *black* Baptist minister west of the Mississippi.

The following is from the archives of the trial and represents what appear to be the notes of the attorney who represented Jacob Perkins,

---

[4] See references to Sandra Loridans and Paul Heinegg.
[5] Kennedy, *The Melungeons*, xviii.
[6] Kennedy, *The Melungeons*, 121.

Thomas A. R. Nelson. The record below is not verbatim. I have tried to make sense of the documents and am including an actual transcription of the text where permitted by the Knox County Public Library. I use footnotes to further illuminate my understanding of the text and included comments regarding points about which I felt strongly.

Finally, it should be noted that in what I believe to be Nelson's Bill of Exceptions there is an implication that Jacob Perkins had African blood. Number 4 of this statement qualifies all of this testimony by saying that if Jacob does not have more than one-eighth Negro or Indian blood, one would be in error to call him a Negro.

Jacob F. Perkins vs. John R. White[7]

Case

> In the cause came the parties by their attornies [*sic*], thereupon came the Jury who were respited from rendering their verdict on yesterday (July 17, 1858), to wit: Ephraim Osburn, Isaac Greer, David Wagner, Jams M. Cable, M. B. Dunn, Washington Cole, David L. Barry, Calaway Elrod, Morgan Smith, Alfred Boasman, Jas. W. M. Grayson & Allen Watson, who upon their oath aforesaid say they find the issue formed in favor of the Defendant. Thereupon the Plaintiff by his Attorney Thos. A. R. Nelson [and?] moves the Court for a new trial, which motion is discharged by the Court. It is thereupon considered by the Court that the Defendant recover of the plaintiff and Joshua Perkins his security of word and in the prosecution bond the costs of this cause for which execution may issue. [Indecipherable] which opinion of the Court in overruling Plffs [Plaintiff's] motion for a new trial and entering Judgment, the Plaintiff prays an appeal to the Superior Court of Errors and Appeals, to be held at the Courthouse in the City of Knoxville on the 2nd Monday in September, which is granted him in having entered into bond of security as required by Law. During the progress

---

[7]My transcriptions below of the various parts of the record are from my reading of the archives of the Nelson Papers in the McClung Collection. In 1998, 1999, and 2000, Pamela R. Cresswell published on the internet her transcription of portions of the records of this trial. Her reading can be found at <http://jctcuzins.com/pam/perkins/index.html>. This "Perkins Trial" internet home page includes Cresswell's introduction and links to the several parts of her transcription: "Trial Notes," "For the Plaintiff," "For the Defendant," "Instructions for the Jury," and "Verdict." Regrettably, Cresswell was very selective and does not provide a complete transcription. Also I have interpreted some of the script differently from her.

of this cause, the plaintiff by his counsel tendered a Bill of Exceptions, which was signed and sealed by the Court and made part of the record.

The following appears to be the Bill of Exceptions included with the decision above. Note the sentence below related to "the plaintiff by his counsel excepts in law." Among the Nelson papers, this section has a cover sheet entitled "J. F. Perkins vs. J. R. White; Nelson's propositions In Charge of the Court."[8]

In the progress of the Trial of this case the Court stated to the jury that no hearsay evidence was to be regarded by them except upon the subject of pedigree or blood of the plaintiffs. They might look to the general reputation of the pedigree or race of the plaintiff, and his ancestors lineal and collateral, and to declarations of deceased persons who were acquainted with him and his ancestors as to their pedigree or race, color and general appearance as to their opinions as to plaintiffs' pedigree or race, found through inspection and acquaintance as to color, general appearance and pedigree.

To the foregoing instructions of the Court given during the progress of the cause, the plaintiff by his counsel excepts in law.

During the whole progress of the cause the plaintiff, by his counsel, objected, as it was introduced, to all of the evidence set out in this bill of exceptions, and the depositions annexed which contain the opinions of the various witnesses examined as to the blood or race of the plaintiff & his relatives lineal and collateral, where such opinions were founded merely upon inspection. Plaintiff, by his counsel, in like manner objected as it was introduced to all the evidence in this cause of the general and common reputation as to the pedigree of the plaintiff. and his said relatives, and insisted that no proof of common reputation or hearsay as to pedigree could be admitted, except where the hearsay was derived from members of the family, that is the relatives lineal and collateral of the plaintiff. And to the action of the court in permitting the evidence above mentioned, as being objected to, to go to the jury, the plaintiff by his counsel excepts in law.

The plaintiff by his counsel also excepts to the rejection of the South Carolina transcript herein before mentioned.

His Honor excluded from the jury so much of the deposition of Anna Graves as details the conversation, of Jock Perkins in regard to his services and those of his sons in the Revolutionary War and also so much as related to George Perkins's discharge because the said proof was mainly hearsay as

---

[8]Thomas A. R. Nelson, "J. F. Perkins vs. J. R. White; Nelson's Propositions In Charge of the Court" (Knoxville TN: Knox County Library, 1858).

to a particular fact, and this action, the court, the plaintiff by his counsel excepts.

The court also excluded from the jury all the evidence contained in this bill of exceptions and the exhibits thereto of hearsay of particular facts and to this action of the court the plaintiff excepts.

Among other things the plaintiff by his counsel requested the Honorable court to instruct the jury as follows:

1. That the statements of members of family from which plaintiff is descended, in regard to this grievance, are better and more reliable than hearsay evidence of common reputation as to pedigree because the family are more deeply interested in preserving a knowledge of their descent.

2. That most in grade to their statements, the family is the evidence of contemporaries of the plaintiff's ancestors as to their pedigree.

3. That mere evidence of opinion as to pedigree of the plaintiff is less reliable than that of the knowledge of members of the family as derived from the statements made prior to any litigation.

4. That if the great-grandfather of plaintiff was an Indian or a Negro, and he is descended on the maternal side from a white woman, without any further Negro or Indian blood than such as he derived on the father's side, then the plaintiff is not of mixed blood, or within the third generation inclusive. In other words that if the plaintiff does not have in his veins more than one-eighth of Negro or Indian blood, he is a citizen of this state and it would be erroneous to call him a Negro.

5. That if it appears from the record that the plaintiffs, ancestors and collateral kindred have exercised the rights of citizenship in voting at elections, acting as jurors, being witnesses in suits between white men, marrying and living with white women, filling civil offices, and sending their children to common schools for more than twenty years, such enjoyment of the rights & privileges of a free white citizen of this state is primary and conclusive proof that the plaintiff is entitled to all the rights and privileges of a free white citizen of this state.

But His Honor refused in all respects to charge the jury as above requested and instructed them as follows,

[Notes of Court's Instructions to the Jury]

Jacob F. Perkins	}	Charge of the Court
vs.	}	
John R. White	}	

The court among other things instructed the jury as follows: Persons that are known and recognized by the Constitution and laws of Tennessee, as free persons of color are those who by the act of 1794, Sec. 32, are taken and deemed to be incapable in law to be witnesses in any case whatever, except against each other. Or in the language of the Statue, "all Negroes, Indians, mulattoes, and all persons of mixed blood descended from Negro or indian ancestors to the third generation <u>inclusive</u> though one ancestor of each generation may have been a white person, whither bond or free." The Statue includes as witnesses those only who are citizens of the Negro or Indian blood or a mixture of both and who fall within the third generation <u>inclusive</u>. To make one then a free person of color one-eighth of his or her entire blood must be either of the Negro or of the Indian races, or a mixture of the two, amounting to one-eighth, to illustrate what is meant by the language of the statute "To the third generation inclusive, though one ancestor of each generation may have been a white person." If the proof in this case shows that Jock Perkins was the great-grandfather of Plaintiff on the paternal line and that with a pure blooded white woman Jacob was produced, Jacob would be of the first generation, one-half of whose blood would be Negro, and Jacob cohabited with a full-blooded white woman and produced Joshua Perkins, to wit Joshua would be the second generation, one-fourth of whose blood would be Negro. And if Joshua and a full-blooded white woman produced the plaintiff, then the plaintiff would be the third generation inclusive, and one-eighth of his blood of the Negro race, and a person of color. If however, the great-grandfather Jock Perkins was less than a Negro of the full blood, then the plaintiff would be less than one-eighth Negro and not a person of color, unless he may have derived a sufficiency of Indian or Negro blood from some of his other ancestors on either of the paternal or maternal lines to make up the deficit. The court further instructed the jury that the statements and declarations of the Plaintiff's ancestors and kindred, respecting their pedigree and blood, was competent testimony before them. That like all other testimony in the cause, it was their province and duty to weigh it and give to each and every part of it such consideration and effect as they in their judgement might think it entitled to receive. The presumption is that the ancestors and family relations of the plaintiff would be most correctly informed as to their and his blood and pedigree. Where there were no suspicions to their motives in making representations concerning their pedigree and the races from which they sprang, more weight should be give to their statements then to those who are unconnected with the family. But the jury might look to the circumstances that surrounded them at the time. If they perceived a strong motive and feeling of interest prompting them to misrepresent their blood and pedigree and to produce a false fame and reputation on the subject, it would so far weaken the force of the testimony and they should give it like credit. On the other hand if the representations were made against the interest and predilections of the persons making them, that circumstances would add to the force and effect of the testimony and the jury should give it more weight and credit.

The court also instructed the jury that the privileges of the citizen which the plaintiff and his ancestors had enjoyed as voters, jurors, witnesses, public officers, marrying and giving in marriage with white persons, and the like, and the length of time that their high privileges had been so enjoyed, were facts and circumstances to which they could look in making up their verdict upon the question of the plaintiffs' blood, and they should receive due consideration. But if after looking to all the testimony, the jury should be satisfied that the plaintiff is a person of color, within the description before given, these privileges, no matter how long enjoyed by him and his ancestors, would not <u>constitute</u> him a citizen and their verdict should be for the defendant.

The court charged upon other questions in the cause but the foregoing is the only part of the charge to which exception was taken by the plaintiff's counsel.

Also charged that the opinion of witnesses founded upon mere observation or inspection as to blood or pedigree is less reliable than the proof of facts from which the jury can determine these questions for themselves.

And to the action of his Honor in neglecting to charge the law as herein before requested and in giving the foregoing instructions to the jury, as well as to his refusal to grant a new trial the plaintiff by his counsel excepts in law and tenders this his bill of exceptions which he prays may be signed and sealed by the court and made part of the record which is done accordingly.

17th July 1855   [Judge] J. M. Melcker [seal]

[Witnesses for the plaintiff][9]

Catharine Roller, aged 80, thought that the Old Jock looked half-white.
David R. Kennick, aged 77, stated he had known the family for 49 years. He said that Jacob's color was a little darker than Joshua's. He also stated that he had never heard the family referred to as anything but Portuguese.
Sarah Kennick, aged 75, testified she had known the Perkins family for 40 years. Although their skin color was dark, they had always been called Portuguese.

[9]All of the depositions are from the notes of Thomas A. R. Nelson, attorney for the plaintiff, in the Perkins file, among the Nelson Papers, in the McClung Collection.

Thomas Cook, aged 75, knew Old Jock Perkins. He described him as a dark-skinned man. He stated that Old Jock resembled an Indian and was generally called Portuguese.

Elizabeth Cook, at 71 years of age, stated she had never seen Old Jock. However, she had heard family testimony that they (the Perkins) were Portuguese. Under cross-examination, Ms. Cook said she heard her mother say that George Perkins's wife told her that she hated it when she went home and found Old Jock was a "colored man." She did not say he was a Negro.

Nancy Young, aged 66 years, stated that she knew George Perkins. "My father and mother knew the Perkins in South Carolina and always said they were Portuguese and the mother a white woman."

John J. Wilson, about 70, testified that he "knew the great-grandfather of plaintiff, old Jock." He described his as dark-skinned with bushy, long hair. His wife was said to be a Scotch woman. On cross-examination, Wilson admitted that some of Jock's neighbors called him a Negro and that Jock's family called themselves Portuguese. Wilson proceeded on to make a reference to the fact that Old Jock's wife did not buy him. Under cross-examination, the witness stated that Old Jock was generally considered Portuguese until someone disagreed with him.

Harry Wilson testified that he was well acquainted with Jock Perkins. He was considered to be "a yellow man—said to be Portuguese." He thought the Perkins did not look like Negroes.

James I. Tipton, aged 65, stated that he had known Joshua Perkins and his brother for 40 or 50 years. During cross-examination, Mr. Tipton said that some people called them Negroes and others called the Perkins Portuguese.

Samuel Vance, aged 64, stated his father in law, Johnson Hampton, said the Perkins were not Negroes; they were Portuguese. During cross-examination, Mr. Vance said he did not believe the family was pure white. He believed they were Portuguese.

Peter Snyder, aged 55, testified that he knew George Perkins, uncle of Joshua. He lived at his father's place when he was a boy. He stated that George was a little darker than Joshua, but did not look like a Negro. He had straight hair.

Hyla Vance, aged 57, stated that she knew the Plaintiff's grandfather. Her description included a high "Roman" nose, dark skin and curly hair, though not kinky. She saw the Jacob at his death. His wife said they were Portuguese.

Bedent Beard, aged 88, knew the paternal grandfather of the Plaintiff also. He was not a Negro according to the witness. He stated that his hair was more like an Indian, than a Negro. The family had lived not far above the mouth of Roan Creek. He said he had known them for 40 years and by reputation for 60 years. They had the privileges of white people, and his wife was a white woman.

Anna Graves, 77 years of age, had her testimony taken in Superior. She appears to be related to the Perkins in some way, perhaps by major. She stated that she knew Jock Perkins. He came from South Carolina in 1785 and died on April 10, 1801. Graves gives the most extensive information, including that Jock Perkins was known to be of the Portuguese race. His wife, Polly, was a white Scotch woman with blue eyes and long brown hair. Her name was Polly Black and Jock had said he married her in 1753. They had six children. Four of his sons fought in the Revolution. She stated that she saw one discharged by General Marion. Two others, Jacob and George, fought against the Indians in 1792. The Perkins stated that they had kept a ferry in South Carolina.

Hardy Graves, aged 64, had his deposition taken in Kentucky. He too claimed to know the great-grandfather, Old Jock. He said that he was always called a Portuguese. Graves knew three of Jock's sons and knew that he had others. He was cognizant of the South Carolina ferry. He added that Jacob Perkins, one of the sons had fought in the battle at Sullivan's Island near Charleston. He saw Jock's discharge. Mr. Graves maintained that the Perkins were not connected to the African race.

Elizabeth Perkins added that she had lived with the family of George Perkins 40 or 50 years ago for 3 months. She confirmed the stories related to the ferry, South Carolina residence, they were mustered into the army and always claimed to be Portuguese. Jacob Perkins, the grandfather of the Plaintiff, was dark-skinned but not African, according to Ms. Perkins.

Sarah Stout, aged 70, was deposed in Lee County. She claimed to have seen Old Jock, the father of Joshua. She said he was a dark-skinned man with a slim face, slim nose and dark-colored hair. In her testimony she stated that he was "as dark-skinned as the blackest of the family." She further stated that all the Perkins were married to white women and were reputed to be Portuguese. During cross-examination, Ms. Stout said that the Perkins family members were not called Negroes, but they were called mulatto by people who were mad at them. This same name calling was applied to the Graves family.

Daniel Stout, as noted earlier, listed four of the sons of Old Jock and the fact that they were called Portuguese. He had lived near them for 40 years. He "never saw old Jock and never heard him called a Negro." According to Mr. Stout, people then did not make such comments.

Martha Shuffield, aged 75, had seen the great-grandfather and thought he looked dark-skinned. She had thought they were Portuguese. "Old Jacob Perkins had nice features & none of them resembled Negroes." She had been his neighbor for 50 years. On cross-examination, Mrs. Shuffield said,

"I saw old Jock through a crib and thought he looked as black as a Negro, but [I] might be mistaken."

According to Nelson's notes, the crux of the depositions for the plaintiff is that the Perkins men were dark-skinned. However, the family story was that they were Portuguese, not African. Furthermore, beginning with Old Jock, the patriarch of this line, each of the Perkins men had married white or Indian women. Thus they became lighter in color in the succeeding generations.

In general, the witnesses said that the Perkins family had associated with general society, had the privileges of the "white" society and had been engaged in lawful business in South Carolina before coming north to Tennessee. The Perkins men had even served in the Revolutionary War and had been mustered during the Indian Wars. The latter is ironic given that there is evidence that they were part Indian and some married women who were part Indian.

The depositions for defendant are next. In general, there is a hard, racist tone to many of the comments. Transcribing this section was extremely difficult. Racism always has created great anxiety for me, but now it is very personal. The names of some of the witnesses are similar to those for the plaintiff, which raises the question of whether members of the same family disagreed. Also there are several witnesses named White. It is unclear if they were related to the defendant.

I have attempted to summarize the comments of the witnesses and add punctuation and correct spelling where necessary. The transcripts of their testimony are available in the McClung Collection, Knox Public Library, Knoxville, Tennessee.

[Deposition for Defendant][10]

David Stout stated that the Perkins family were reputed to be mulattoes, not Portuguese.

H. H. Rhia testified that eighteen months before a J. J. Wilson said that Old Jock was a Negro.

Lilburn C. Berry also testified that twelve to eighteen months before the same J.J. Wilson had said Jock was a Negro. Some years before the witness

---

[10]Again, these abstracts of despositions for the defendant are from the notes of Nelson, Nelson Papers, McClung Collection.

had heard a man named Dugger say that "he would not vote where a
d____d Negro sat as judge. Joshua Perkins'son took it up."[11]

Nicholas Smith stated that he heard "Johnson Hampton say he heard old
man Perkins and Nancy (Graves?) talk of Guineagree."[12]

Nancy Miller testified that Old Jock sold hats. She stated that he was a
black Negro. Under cross-examination, she claimed Jock's wife was with
him, she did not see her face.

Jesse H. White stated that he had known the Perkins for eight years. He
repeated the earlier statement that Johnson Hampton had heard talk among
some of the Perkins that they were Guineagree.

Larkin L. White said he had seen old Jake Perkins. He claimed the man was
a dark mulatto. He also asserted that old Jake had kinky hair.

Celia Goodwin testified that the Perkins were called Negroes. She said she
was well acquainted with the family. One of the Perkins wives said the
"mixture on her side (was) Portuguese and on her husband's negoes [*sic*]"
Mrs. Goodwin stated that William Perkins, the plaintiff's brother was
married to her granddaughter.

Dicey Whaley testified that her mother would not let her socialize with the
Perkins because they were colored. "When people (were) mad, (they) called
them Negroes. (When) Not mad, dark-skinned." On cross-examination, Ms.
Whaley is the first to bring up the issue of smell. She claimed to have been
with the wives and children and been able to smell them.[13]

---

[11]This statement suggests that the dispute did originate from the question of
whether Jacob F. Perkins could serve as an election official because of race.

[12]The reference to *Guinea* or *Guineagree* begins in the transcript here. There are
several possible explanations for this use of this term. In America, Guineas are a
group of triracial people who lived in Maryland and West Virginia, then migrated
to Ohio. West African Guinea-Bissau (previously Gabu) was a Portuguese colony
(mid-fifteenth century until 1879) and (French) Guinea was a French colony
(1849–1958). (The Portuguese may have been the first European slave traders,
especially of blacks from Gabu.) Beginning in the mid-eighteenth century, "Guinea
negro" referred to a person from Guinea; by the early nineteenth century "Guinea"
was used alone (without "negro") to refer to a person of darker coloring and then
of any person of mixed ancestry. This sense of the word, however, is now rare or
obsolete. (As an offensive racial slur, "Guinea" or "Ginnie" was directed against
Italians and their descendants [especially in New York City]—first recorded in
1890—probably inspired by "Guinea" in the sense of a black person with reference
to the relatively dark skin of southern Italians, the majority of Italian immigrants
at the time.)

[13]This testimony opens a door to several witnesses either being asked or offering

<u>Mary White</u> stated that she knew the older Perkins men. According to her, they were very dark-skinned and "always called Negro or Guinea." She stated that "old Richard White said he saw Jacob Perkins's father (Old Jock) on Pedee and he was a Negro." Mrs. White also mentions the smell. However, on cross-examination she states she has slept with the family. The Perkins were treated as "white people" in their house. She also admits that John R. White is her son.

<u>Jane Griffey</u> stated she knew them a year before when she washed William Perkins's clothes. Mrs. Griffey claimed that the clothes smelled like a Negro's. She claimed that she knows the smell of a Negro's clothes.

This profound insight into racism created for me a lot of anger and anxiety. These people were castigated because of their color no matter what the source. The idea of the smell, that deepest level of consciousness, is so incredible. We prove our ideas because we identify a smell? Maybe racism has an odor.

<u>Dr. John E. Copen [Cossen?]</u> testified that he knew the Plaintiff's mother and father. He believed the father to be a Negro. Although his evidence was set aside and he stated that he knew his oath would not be taken, his comments are still recorded in the list of depositions. His general testimony was that he had seen Portuguese people and some of the features of the Jake Perkins were African. He did say that although they were dark-skinned, he was the family doctor and never smelled anything different about them.

<u>John Potter</u>, aged 42, had heard his mother say "old Jock was a kinky-headed Negro and as ugly as ever she saw and thick-lipped." He then related other comments from people about the Perkins and Graves families being called Negroes. It appears that this happened most often after a quarrel.

<u>Reuben Brooks</u> called old Jake "a very black and reverend Negro." He described his features as including a flat nose and kinky hair.

<u>Ellen Anderson</u> stated that she had seen Jacob Perkins and his sons. From her perspective he was a black man.[14] According to Mrs. Anderson the Perkins had always been referred to as Negroes. She makes reference also to a fight over drinking water. Mrs. Anderson also stated that her uncle refused to "make friends with Jock, a d____d Negro son of a bitch."

<u>Nancy Lipps</u> testified that she had known Joe Perkins forty years ago. She described him as a big dark-skinned man with "sheeps wool and flat nose."

---

the idea that the Perkins had a "Negro smell," which was evidence of their race.

[14]For the first time the term "black" was used in testimony.

She stated, "I refused to sleep with a d____d Negro. Old folks said his father was a Negro and came from Pedee. They all looked like Negroes (Josh) & all. I have cursed them to their face."[15]

John D. Shuffield, aged 65, stated that Joshua's father, uncles, and the Graves family were all dark. He testified that his step-grandfather had known the Plaintiff's grandfather in South Carolina. There the Plaintiff's grandfather was called a free man in South Carolina. He also testified that Archibald White said the grandfather was "a blue gum Negro." Joshua's mother was reported said that the Graves family was Portuguese and her brother was Guineagree. Despite this, the family had all the privileges of "white" society.

Sarah Oaks, aged 65, testified as to seeing several members of the family. She stated that Old Jock was said to be Negro. Other family members had dark skin, even though their wives were fair. According to Mrs. Oaks, she believed the Graves family was "mixed blooded." Her brother had "married one of them and his children" were dark.

Goulder Hicks, aged 69, commented on various family members as well. Lewis Perkins was described as "dark and bushy-haired." He knew Ben and Nancy Graves and believed them to be "mixed blooded." (Mr. Hicks stated in his testimony that he prosecuted the Perkins in North Carolina. He also stated that Hannah Perkins, the Plaintiff's cousin, gave sworn testimony. However, it is unclear whether this was an earlier case in reference to this complaint, or a separate unrelated case.

Catherine Wilcox, aged 55, described Old Jake Perkins as a "dark-complected man." She states that his hair was cut close, but it was kinky around the neck.[16]

Thomas Curtis, aged 81 to 82, testified to knowing Jock Perkins in North Carolina 60 years before. He described his as "middling dark." Jock stayed with his family and his parents said he was a free Negro. With cross-examination the witness said he had seen Old Jock numerous times, but he did not remember his features. He also did not know his race.

Harmon Hicks stated that he saw Joshua's father and was afraid of him. He said that the general belief was that the Perkins were "mixed with Negro."

---

[15]A comment at the end of her testimony referred to a fight between her uncle and Joshua Perkins.

[16]The repeated references to "Old Jake" and "Old Jock" are confusing. In trying to sequence the players it seems that Old Jock is the patriarch, the great-grandfather of the plaintiff, Jacob F. Perkins. Old Jake is Jacob Perkins, the grandfather of the plaintiff. A second Joshua, or Josh, is the father of the plaintiff. The repetition of the names led to the same confusion with several generations later in Goliad, Texas.

He apparently was asked about the Graves as well. He stated that Peggy Graves was his sister-in-law, and their marriage had been "objected to." On cross-examination, the witness admitted that he was ten years old when he saw Jacob Perkins. He also answered that the Graves had all the privileges of "white" society.

William Rowland stated that Perkins and Graves were said to be "mixed." He stated that Hiram Hicks, a son of the Graves, had said Old Jock was a Negro.

Joshua Davis's deposition was taken in Marlboro District, South Carolina. He stated that he did not remember the Perkins 60 or 70 years ago.

Henry S. Crabb of Marlboro District stated that he had seen full-blood Portuguese men. He described Portuguese men as muscular and bony with dark skin, gray eyes and auburn hair. He went on to say that "mulattoes generally have kinky hair."[17]

Elisha Smith testified that Jacob Perkins and Mrs. Graves were considered mixed with Negro. According to Smith they were not treated as "white."

John Nave, aged 88, stated that he knew Jock Perkins. He described him as a black man with nappy hair. Nave said the he was called Negro Perkins. He stated that Jacob Perkins was a relation of Jock. According to Nave, some people called Jacob Portuguese and others called him a Negro. To Mr. Nave, Jacob was black and the Graves were the color of Indians. He believed the Graves were mixed.

Mary Thompson, aged 66, stated that a man named Perkins had stayed at her father's house when she was twelve years old. Her mother did not want him there, but her cousin vouched for his respectability. "It was said his father was a slave and saved his master from drowning and his wife, after his death, had a child by him."

Isaac Gwin testified that he had worked with old Jacob. According to him, the Perkins referred to themselves as "dark-skinned or Negroes." He further stated that other people called them the same, and they were not angry about it. His father said that "Old Jock was a kinky-headed Negro." He stated that "Nancy Graves was dark red like a Cherokee. Nancy Graves or Perkins stayed with us 4 or 5 days and said her people were Portuguese & her husband, Negro-gre."

Isaac Reese testified that all of the Perkins looked more like black people than white. He then described various family members ranging in color from dark Negro to mulatto.

---

[17]The testimony seemed to lay the ground for distinguishing between "Africans" and "Portuguese."

George P. Stout at age 87 said that he knew Jacob Perkins and his brothers. They were generally called mulatto.

James Bradley described Jacob as having very dark, nappy hair. He said Jacob was called a Negro. He further testified that George Perkins had said his father was a black man. Bradley went on to list the names of Jacob's children and say they were "called a great many names by the people." He also stated that "John Graves was a colored man. He claimed to have seen four Portuguese and described them. Finally, this witness admitted to being a second cousin to the defendant.

Abner Duncan, 86 years of age, claimed to know Old Jock on the Pedee in North Carolina. He met Jacob Perkins upon coming to Tennessee. According to Duncan, Old Jock was black with kinky hair. He further stated that Jacob was a half-breed with nappy hair. Duncan stated that all of Joshua's children were called Negroes.

He also stated that John Graves called himself a big Negro.[18]

John Estrep, aged 74, testified to having seen Old Jock. He described him as a very dark man. He said his hair was kinky. He also stated that Jacob and his family were called mulattoes. On cross-examination, the witness admitted that he was related to Mr. Dugger, one of the defendants.

William Overby, aged 72, said he had seen Jock Perkins once. He described him as dark-skinned with kinky hair. He said the family were called Negroes, although the wife was described as white.

William Garland, aged 75, that he knew Jacob and George Perkins, as well as John Graves. He said the Perkins were reported to be mulatto.

Thomas Elliot, aged 90, testified he knew Jacob Perkins and his brothers. He reported more about kinky hair and quote John Grindstaff as saying that "Jock was as black as his Negro Jim." Elliott stated that he had never seen Jock.

Lewis Lewis saw old Jake Perkins, the grandfather, Joshua's father. He called him a Guinea. He stated that "Jack Perkins hair was woolly as wool on a sheep's back."

Elizabeth Heatherly stated that she knew old Jock Perkins. She had heard that old Jock's father was a mulatto.

Catharine Patterson, aged 38, testified that William Perkins smell was not different but she did not want him staying at her house because he was too dark in color.

---

[18]A comment in the margins of the notes reads "Manure." Since it is underlined twice, it appears to express Nelson's frustration with the testimony.

I sit here filled with the grief at the injustice of the world, but mostly the injustice of racism and bigotry. The next portion of these notes are so painful that I needed to pour out the feelings of indignity, of anger, of horror at what was said. These people, these Perkins, are my people. All of this spitefulness and hatred is a result of the otherness related to color. Or was color used as an excuse for perpetrating and intensifying hatred? How could this have happened?

If I was horrified at what I had read so far, the remainder of the depositions, which were separate from those carried before, had the effect of piercing my innermost core. I have struggled with the face of deceit, poverty, starvation, and injustice in the world, but nothing prepared me for the outrage and pain of these final passages.

The inscription at the edge of the following two paragraphs is beside a large bracket. The words read "White alone." Since this case was between Jacob F. Perkins and John R. White, I presume this is the man referred to in the inscription. Unlike the other passages, I have left these intact, complete with misspellings and poor grammar. The effect of reading them as they were recorded is much more powerful.

[According to Goodwin,] White said he had sold his damaged old Negro Frank Perkins for fives dollars and had the money in his pocket. He said we have put one old Negro by his oath and at the next court the work will be done for the balance. And he said old Josh could trade no more only what he rased [sic] on his farm. He said all the Perkins would or should be indited next court for livin [sic] with their wives.

Robert L. Goodwin

[Hamby testified that] I was talking with Tom Copper about a wagon I bought of J. F. Perkins. White was by and said to me he would put me up for trading with his Negroes without his leave. I said I did not no [sic] it. He said you know it now. He asked me what I gave for the wagon. I told him. He said he believed he would let me off as long as I gave a fare [sic] price.

Thomas Hamby

The next section of testimony is with regard to "White and wife."

White's wife said to Perkins I understand you will not let my Negroes come here and he said they should not. And she said they should come where they please. One Negrow [sic] had privledges [sic] to go where others was and her Negrows should come there. And she dare him to whip them.

White came rushing up with his gun and Perkins started into his house. And White said look how stable the damed old Negrow dobbin walks.
[Unsigned or part of following?]

Jim Dugger said to me that old Joshua Perkins grandfather was a cole [*sic*] black Negrow. And he intended to put all the Perkins by their oath. And if he succeeded as he wish to he would inditt [*sic*] them every court for living with their wives. He said what made their hair strate [*sic*] was the Indian in Kite.[19] We was talking about Josh Perkins and he Dugger said tell the old Negrow he need not trouble him self to go to the speaking for he did not intend he should vote.
    Alfred N. Greenwill

Dugger said to me they were going to have a speaking at the forge to see if the Perkins had souls or no. And if it was apertained that they had not souls, he would take his gun and go down. And asked me if I would go with. My best impression that he said he would go down and kill them. He said he had them in fare [*sic*] way to put them all by their oath. And he intended to stop till he done it if he could.
    Isaac Moody

The following piece of Nelson's notes is harder to read and has been pieced together.

[Illegible: Dugger?] said to me he had put old Josh Perkins by his oath and he intended [illegible] at the next court if he could. He say they were going to have a speaking at the forge to see if the Perkins had souls or not. If not, he allowed to take his gun and go down and kill a parsell [*sic*] of them. He said they were like mules. Mules was [illegible] breeding and these molotters [*sic*] when mix that far had no souls.
    John Moody

Jacob Perkins lost his case and was required to pay all court fees. He would appeal to the district court, and according to some historians he won the case. Another researcher states that a further appeal by the defendants resulted in Jacob Perkins losing the case. Although there is no account available analyzing the effects of these legal actions, descendants of Jacob Perkins have enjoyed all the privileges of white citizens in Tennessee.

---

[19]Elizabeth Kite was married to one of the Perkins. She has been identified in family records as "Indian."

As for Thomas A. R. Nelson, modern researchers have hailed him as a hero for his legal efforts on behalf of Jacob Perkins. His notes indicate one particular legal issue. What is "mixed" blood? How do we calculate percentage of race? Is it important? Other cases over the years and practices by state legal entities would try to define the same question.

A completely different atmosphere exists today. Census records now allow for a "mixed" category on their forms. Many people claim with pride their mixed heritage. But for those of us who do not know about our racial makeup, it is not even a question. For the descendants of Old Jock, we will ask the question of where he came from.

Oh Esther, "Beautifully formed and lovely to behold,"[1]
Who fathered your lovely children?
Did he know that they would live
outside the bounds of convention for a time?
Did you feel despair at their birth
or did you celebrate the miracle of their births?
Did you anticipate the legacy that you were creating
with the creation of each life?
Did you know the tiny ones were destined to be orphans?
And bound into servitude into adulthood?
Did you weep with anguish and grief?
Or did you raise your chin with pride
And know that they would flourish?
You defied convention by giving birth
To life
To a future
To a new generation
Of people blended with the best of the continents.
Did you know your son would become a weaver?
Of a tapestry of mystery?
Their father must have been Grandfather Spider.

---

[1]Esther 2:7 (New American Bible).

Chapter 7

The Myth of the Missing Father

Throughout the generations history demonstrated a recurring phenomenon. Fathers seemed to be absent or to disappear from the lives of their children. Missing fathers were not unusual during wars or modern-day work that occurred in cities. Among rural families, however, fathers were always present. Even in my own generation, my siblings and I each first married men and women who did not have fathers present in their lives. In the case of my first husband, his father died when he was ten years old. My current husband had a father present in the household, but he was extremely reclusive and the mother was the real parent for the children.

My paternal grandfather died when my father was six years old. My father was always traveling and was not home when any of us were born. Because of divorce and introverted spouses, all of the children of my daughters' generation, their cousins, have grown up without a father in their daily lives. My granddaughter is growing up in a household with a single female parent.

As my husband and I searched the backgrounds of the Perkins family, it is clear that they lived the lives of cowboys and stockmen. The lifestyle of movement and being in the fields may have meant a lot of time away from home. Were these fathers part of their children's lives? Perhaps the record of Jordan Perkins and his sons is one of staying together more than being apart. However, the missing-father story pervades the history of this family.

The debate over "Old Jock's" parentage has formed a part of the mystery of the Perkins family. One "cousin" believes "Old Jock" was the son of Richard Perkins and Mary Sherrill. Richard and his brother, Elisha, were found by various records to have been settled in Baltimore County, Maryland in 1741.[1] The Perkins brothers were the sons of Richard Perkins and Mary Utie. Richard, Sr. was said to have come from England. Richard, Jr. and Elisha Perkins had sons named Joshua. The first was born in 1730 in Baltimore County, Maryland. The second son was born to Elisha Perkins and Margaret Sherrill (possibly a sister of Mary). This Joshua was born in 1728.

Because of the later controversy of "Old Jock's" skin color, a third Joshua Perkins is the more likely candidate. He first appeared in 1734 Accomack County court orders.[2] In January 2001, we set out on a daylong trip to the eastern shore of Maryland and the Virginia peninsula, which juts down into the Atlantic Ocean. There we retrieved a series of documents that provided more questions then answers.

On the eighth of July, 1730, Thomas Blair, a gentleman of the court, paid the fine of Esther Perkins "for having a Bastard Child."[3] Esther's ethnicity is not noted in this set of orders, even though other orders make such classification. However as early as 1691, Virginia's colonial legislature and General Assembly passed a law that "if any English woman being free shall have a bastard child by a Negro she shall pay fifteen pounds to the church wardens."[4] Historians have assumed that Esther may have been a white servant woman who had a child by an African slave.[5] However, the father could have been a free Negro, and the union could have been any marriage unrecognized by colonial law. Later laws would become much harsher with regard to intermarriage or sex between blacks and whites, especially where the woman was white and the man black.[6]

The next Perkins who shows up on the Accomack County records is Joshua Perkins. On August 13, 1734, the court ordered that "Joshua Perkins orphan aged two years & Darky Perkins orphan aged six years be bound to James Gibson he teaching the Boy the Trade of Weaver & performing to

---

[1]Thomas Perkins, unpublished family history (1998) 4.

[2]Heinegg, *Free African Americans*, 546.

[3]June Purcell Gould, *Black Laws of Virginia* (Lovettsville VA: Willow Bend Books, 1996) 24.

[4]Ibid.

[5]Heinegg, *Free African Americans*, 1.

[6]See Lawrence Tenzer's excellent work on interracial issues in colonial history: *A Completely New Look at Interracial Sexuality* (Manahawkin NJ: Scholars Publishing House, 1990). See also Tenzer's *The Forgotten Cause of the Civil War: A New Look at the Slavery Issue* (Manahawkin NJ: Scholars Publishing House, 1997).

both the said orphans what the Law enjoyns."[7] In 1705, the state of Virginia had designated in dealing with orphans that "the church wardens shall bind the child to be a servant until it shall be thirty-one years of age."[8] The indentured status of Joshua Perkins implies an apprenticeship, as do many of the other records in the Accomack County court records. Joshua and Darky were probably brother and sister. Were Darky and Dorcas, who appears later in the records, the same person?

On January 27, 1746, the courts dropped an action of debt brought by the church wardens against Dorcas Perkins. The reason for dropping the action was that Dorcas had died.[9] It is possible that Dorcas was the same as Darky. She would have been 18 years old. Further confusion occurs when the June 8, 1748 records state that Jacob, "a Mulatto Boy son of Esther Perkins (deceased) aged two years last Christmas be bound by the Church Wardens of Accomack Parish to Geo. Bundick Jr. to learn the Trade of Shoemaker."[10] Esther was presumably already deceased if she was the mother of Joshua and Darky (Dorcas).

Then on June 28, 1748 another entry provides the following citation: "Ordered that Jacob a Mulatto Boy Orphan Son of Darky Perkins Deceased. Aged two years next Christmas be bound by the Church Wardens of the Parish of Accomack to James Gibson till Lawful age to learn the Trade of Shoemaker."[11]

Are these two boys the same? The action of debt against Darky was most likely for having a child illegitimately. Either the father of Jacob was African or Darky was considered mulatto herself. Her son, Jacob, was born around Christmas and the earlier entry as to his mother could have been a mistake. It seems logical for him to be bound out to James Gibson who also had Joshua, Jacob's uncle, and Darky, Jacob's mother, in servitude.

Paul Heinegg believes Esther's children included Darky or Dorcas, Joshua, George, Jacob, and Arcadia. If Esther was dead by 1734 when Darky or Dorcas and Joshua were bound out as orphans, she could not be the mother of George, Jacob, and Arcadia. These individuals were all born after her presumed death. Jacob could have been the child of Darky, as the

---

[7]Accomack County Virginia Orders 1744–1753, 133.
[8]Gould, *Black Laws of Virginia*, 26.
[9]Accomack County Virginia Orders 1744–1753, 181.
[10]Accomack County Virginia Orders 1744–1753, 273.
[11]Accomack County Virginia Orders 1744–1753, 280.

county records support. Arcadia, aged six, was bound to George Hoyetil in
1752.[12] She could have been Darky's daughter, depending on the time of
year she was born. However, another child, Jemmy, was four years old in
1752 when he was bound out to learn the trade of shoemaker to the same
George Hoyetil.[13] It is more likely that Jemmy and Arcadia were siblings. All
the Perkins above were specifically described in the records as "mulattos."[14]

Thomas Blair paid Esther Perkins's fines for her in 1730. He appears in
the court as one of the judges or jurors. Who was Thomas Blair and why
would he pay her fine? Was he the father of her children? Was she a servant
girl for the Blair household? Did one of his slaves father her children? These
questions are unanswered. Accomack County holds records relating to
Thomas Blair, specifically his will and an inventory of his possessions at the
time of his death.

Thomas Blair was a wealthy merchant who owned property in Virginia
and Maryland. Since his will included bequests to his mother and brother
in Glasgow, it is assumed he came to the coastline of the colonies from
Scotland.[15] Blair was married to Anne Makemie, the daughter of a Scottish
minister. They had no children upon his death in 1740. Whether he was the
father of Esther's children is doubtful. The children were presumed mulatto,
and Blair was white. However, why did he pay Esther's fine?

Blair did own slaves. At the time of his death, there are forty-two slaves
listed by first name only. Among those names are Nimrod and Dorcas.
These names appear later in lists of free-negro Perkins, but they could have
been just common names of the times. Without any other theories, Paul
Heinegg's seems as acceptable as any others. Heinegg postulates that Esther
was a white servant girl who had children with a Negro slave. In accordance
with law, she was fined and her children bound out. The children may have
stayed with her for a time because they were not bound out until her death,
if these records are correct.[16]

By 1800, a number of Perkins appeared in the U.S. census for
Accomack Parish and St. George's Parish. Since it was the law to enumerate

---

[12]Accomack County Virginia Orders 1744–1753, 570.
[13]Heinegg, *Free African Americans*, 545.
[14]Heinegg, *Free African Americans*, 545-48.
[15]Thomas Blair, Last Will & Testament (Accomack County VA, September 12, 1739) 214-15.
[16]Heinegg, *Free African Americans*, 1.

free Blacks,[17] the records provide evidence of Perkins's ethnicity. In Accomack Parish, Nimrod Perkins headed a household of nine persons. Kiah Perkins also headed a household of nine. In St. George's Parish, there were three Perkins households. Comfort Perkins was the head of a household of five free Blacks, and there were two households headed by Esther Perkins.[18] One had three members; the other had four. Are all these the descendants of the first Esther? It seems plausible.

An alternative scenario also exists. In the Tennessee trial, Mary Thompson relates a curious story. "It was said his father [Old Jock] was a slave and saved his master from drowning and his wife, after his death, had a child by him."[19] If Esther Perkins had been a widow and fathered children by a slave, she would still have been required to pay the fine and have her children "bound" to tradesmen and farmers upon her death.

What happened to Esther's children? Darky or Dorcas died in Accomack County, if the records are correct. Seven possible children are listed in various records. George Perkins was listed as a "mulatto" servant of James Gibson as late as 1751. He may be the same George Perkins who appeared in the Carolinas as a soldier and landholder. Since Joshua went to the Carolinas, it was possible that this George was his brother.

Joshua Perkins purchased land in Bladen County, North Carolina at Wilkerson Swamp on the Pee Dee River in 1768.[20] The purchase was fully within the time frame of when he would have completed his servitude. In addition, this land was half of a tract owned by Robert Sweat, a name quite familiar to this research. Old Jock's son, Joshua, testified that he was born on the Pee Dee River and had lived most of his life near Gilbert Sweat.[21]

Joshua would marry Mary Black, who was said to be a white woman, and go on to manage a ferry, raise many children, and continue to carry the stigma of his skin color. I am convinced that Esther was his mother and wonder what it must have been like for her to love a man and never have the life of a family. Did she have faith that times would change? Did she

---

[17]Guild, *Black Laws of Virginia*, 26.
[18]U.S. Bureau of Census, Accomack and St. George Parishes VA, 1800, 17-19.
[19]Thomas A. R. Nelson, notes for *Jacob F. Perkins vs. John R. White*, 1858.
[20]Bladen County North Carolina Land Deeds, no. 1210, 1768.
[21]*Delaney vs. Swett*, District Court No. 1533, St. Landry Parish, Opelousas LA, 1830.

pray that life would give her children the blessings she could not? Did she hope that in generations to come the pain of separation would heal?

The Path of Creation

Chapter 8 explores the origins of triracial peoples, with reference to many other groups besides the Red Bones. It celebrates some of the possibilities for the origins of my people. Despite the insistence of those who favor a more European and Native American story, I accept the strong indications that part of our heritage comes from Africa. I have placed this chapter in the Path of Creation because I believe it was due to their creativity that these people found a way to meld into society and make a contribution. Whether assimilation was their intent is unknown. My guess is they mainly wanted to be free to conduct their own affairs.

Chapter 9 looks more closely at that creativity and the cultural inputs of the "cowpenner" or "cowboy." In particular I seek to examine the connection to the land that these people had, and the inheritance they gave to us, their descendants. In this situation both the paternal "power" and the maternal "symbolic totems of nature" come into play as part of the Path of Creation.

The third path continues into chapter 10. Here I have tried to examine the gifts of three spiritual traditions: Christian, African, and Native American. Specifically I try to identify what I have inherited from each of these spiritual approaches. In this chapter, I begin to step into the Path of Transformation.

In *Original Blessing*, the great German mystic Meister Eckhart is quoted as saying we find the equality of God within ourselves in the Creativa.[1] The people I am recovering found a way to survive and thrive in the world. Their lives were filled with story and music. They had large families that met the promise of spreading across the landscape. Over the decades to come they would be known for their sense of community. From poverty and racism to the lasting hope of wonder, the Perkins family birthed a future.

---

[1] Fox, *Original Blessing*, 187.

Shipwrecked upon an eastern coastline?
Or brought aboard a slave ship?
Lost tribe or stolen tribes of men and women
Longing for the land where your ancestors roamed?
What was your native language?
Bacongo, Wolof, Lunda, Ovimbundu, Portuguese, Arabic?
And did you use Cherokee, Choctaw
Or one of the ancient lost tongues of the Powhatan Confederacy?
I may never know
Except that somewhere in the whirlwind
I have Spirit, a da nv to and Life, v le ni to nv.

Chapter 8

The Mystery of Our Origins

The origins of the Red Bones or Redbone people requires mastering a puzzle whose pieces are flung across the landscape. Very little has been written about this specific triracial group. What has been published is often filled with more supposition than fact. The best way to unravel the entangled strands of history and oral tradition seemed to be to once again go backward in time and review each of the theories presented by major researchers. Attempts to divide the approaches to this research into several basic theories were important to finding the truth. However, at times the theories overlap. In the end, I make my own guesses about who we are and where we came from.

Various researchers have taken different approaches and their theories fall into overlapping areas. The first three approaches are based on ethnology and genealogy. The fourth is the work of a geographer and historian.

The Melungeon theory has received much publicity due to the work of Brent Kennedy. His work is a combination of family history and scientific research. The work of Virginia DeMarce and Gary Mills is focused on triracial isolates and has strong genealogical research combined with historical overlay. The third category relates to the early African-American research compiled by Paul Heinegg. Heinegg has exhaustively collected and organized old records from the earliest days of colonial America. Finally, the cowpen heritage documented by Terry G. Jordan provides unique insight into the tradition of cattlemen from its origins to the movement west. There are a few other writers on the subject, but their work fits into one or more of these categories.

Melungeons are identified as a group of people found largely in the Appalachian Mountains, specifically at Newman's Ridge in Hancock County, Tennessee. They have specific characteristics, including clearly identified names and some similar physical traits. Whether Melungeons are a distinct racial group is a topic of controversy. The source of the term "Melungeon" is also in question. Some theories are that the word comes from the French *melange* meaning "mixture." Others claim that *melungo*, meaning "shipmate" or "companion," comes from an Afro-Portuguese word.[1] However, there are theorists who point to the name *Goins*—sometimes spelled Goen, Gowens, Gawain, and other variations—as the source of the Melungeon group of people who were of mixed race.

In the two most common books on Melungeons, almost every author relates a story of dark-skinned people who may have been surviving descendants of the "Lost Colony" of Roanoke Island.[2] In the late 1500s England established a colony off the coast of North Carolina on Roanoke Island. In 1587, Governor John White left the colony to sail back to England, leaving his family behind. According to historians, Governor White's return was delayed for three years. When a ship finally arrived at the colony, they found it abandoned. However,

> one of the chiefe trees or postes at the right side of the entrance had the barke taken off, and 5. Foote from the ground in fayre Capitall letters was graven CROATOAN without a crosse or signe of distress.[3]

The rescuers assumed that the colonists had been unable to survive the stormy coastline and had gone to live with the local Indians. The colonists were never found, and the mystery remains as to their fate. The triracial tribe of Lumbee Indians, who live in Robeson County, North Carolina have an oral tradition from one elder that his ancestors came from Roanoke, Virginia.[4] The Perkins name exists among the Nansemond tribe, which was located near Suffolk, Virginia when Jamestown was settled in 1607. The Nansemond tribe is one of the few remaining members of the Powhatan Confederacy and is today located in Chesapeake, Virginia.

In the 1880s, Hamilton McMillan advanced another theory that connected the Roanoke Colony with mixed-race persons in North Carolina. According to this story, McMillan was living in North Carolina near the Lumbee Indians of Robeson County. He lived "near a settlement of 'persons

---

[1]Jean Patterson Bible, *Melungeons Yesterday and Today* (Signal Mountain TN: Mountain Press, 1975) 11.

[2]Bonnie Ball, *The Melungeons* (Johnson City TN: Overmountain Press, 1992) vii-viii; Kennedy, *The Melungeons*, 81.

[3]David Stick, *Roanoke Island: The Beginnings of English America* (Chapel Hill NC: University of North Carolina Press, 1983) 210.

[4]Stick, *Roanoke Island: The Beginnings of English America*, 241.

of mixed color,' sometimes known as 'red bones' and long classed as mulattoes, though recognized locally as Indians." The people were refused entry into white schools, and according to the story they refused to attend Negro schools.[5] McMillan further reported that there were some people who spoke an old English dialect. He became convinced that these people were descendants of the Lost Colony. He was so sure that he had a bill enacted in the 1885 North Carolina General Assembly session to provide "schools for Croatan Indians in Robeson County."[6]

In 1997, we visited the courthouse in Bladen County, North Carolina. We were copying land deeds that recorded the transactions conducted by "Old Jock" Perkins. While in the courthouse, we were approached by a young man named Lamar Corbett. Lamar is the tribal genealogist for the Waccamaw Indians. He looks like an African-American Indian, carrying traits of both, but he has lighter skin and deep blue eyes. Lamar said that the Waccamaw are often lumped with the Cherokee. However, there are several Indian tribes in the area: Cape Fear, Pedee, Cheraws, Waccamaw, and Lumbee. According to Lamar, there are Perkins families among the Waccamaw. The Lumbee Indians are the best known in the area. Whether they are descendants of the Roanoke Colony, however, is unproven. Many historians believe the remains of the colony were lost at sea while trying to return to England.[7]

Another theory connects the Melungeons as descendants of Carthage who arrived centuries before other discoveries of the Western Hemisphere. This explanation dovetails with N. Brent Kennedy's connection to the Mediterranean coastline, although he has focused on Turkey as the source. However, the Carthaginian argument gained prominence because of another Tennessee court case, this one in 1872. A young woman seeking to lay claim to an inheritance had to prove that her Melungeon mother was not Negro. Under Tennessee law, miscegenation was the marriage of a white person with one of Negro blood to the sixth degree,[8] and one carrying this amount of Negro blood could not inherit from a white father. The lawyer for the young woman relied upon the traditions of the Melungeons that their

---

[5]Stick, *Roanoke Island: The Beginnings of English America*, 231.
[6]Stick, *Roanoke Island: The Beginnings of English America*, 232.
[7]Stick, *Roanoke Island: The Beginnings of English America*, 235-36.
[8]Bible, *Melungeons Yesterday and Today*, 61.

people had come from Carthage to Portugal and then to the coast of South and North Carolina.[9] He was successful in winning his case.

Another writer makes a case for Moorish influence. She even lists some common characteristics between Moors and Melungeons. They have similar physical features: fine noses, dark skin, black hair. They were present in Spain and Portugal and had to flee. Many lived in the mountains. Both groups were herders of livestock.[10] The latter characteristic is particularly of interest because of the occupation of my own family members. However, it is interesting to note that the Perkins were for the most part not mountain dwellers. Many present-day "Melungeon" families do live in the mountains.

The most persistent reference to ethnic background among the Melungeons is Portuguese. The Moor and Carthaginian theories would not rule out the Portuguese. However, another theory often mentioned is that of the shipwrecked Portuguese sailor.[11] The primary argument against a direct Portuguese link is the lack of Portuguese names in the family and the inclination of most of the families to be Protestant. However, it becomes confusing because Portuguese colonies were also in Africa. In *Jacob F. Perkins vs. John R. White*, there are several references to Guinea and Guineagree. Does this refer to Guinea, a part of West Africa, which was partly colonized by the Portuguese? Guinea stretches along the shore between Senegal and Cape Negro.

Virginia DeMarce's work is that of a historian and genealogist. Her article for the National Genealogical Society opened the door to further study of triracial people, which were classified as "isolates" by anthropologists.[12] DeMarce specifically identifies Red Bones and the Perkins family as one of the triracial isolates, as does her colleague, Gary Mills, in a later article.

In addition, both authors point out the strong possibilities of intermarriage between whites and Indians, whites and Africans, and Africans and Indians. DeMarce identifies the tendency to live in marginal locations and sites where they were accepted. When that acceptance became compromised,

---

[9]Bible, *Melungeons Yesterday and Today*, 64.
[10]Ball, *The Melungeons*, 27.
[11]Kennedy, *The Melungeons*, 83.
[12]Virginia Easley DeMarce, " 'Very Slitly Mixt': Triracial Isolate Families of the Upper South—A Genealogical Study," *National Genealogical Society Quarterly* 80 (March 1991): 5-35.

the families struck out for new locations.[13] In the case of the Perkins, one line seemed to go into the Midwest and the other to the South.

In DeMarce's research, the Perkins name appears early in historical documents in conjunction with Nansemond Indians. Given that the Nansemond tribe still exists in Virginia not too far from Accomack County, a possible source for early intermarriage could have been within that tribe.

While it is difficult to exactly trace the African origins, Perkins family members did marry Goins family members. Jordan Perkins married Virginia Jane Goen/Goins, and two of his sisters married two of her brothers. There seems to be no question that the Goins patriarch is Mihill Goen (Michael Gowen), a Negro who was given his freedom after the death of his master in 1657.[14]

Gary Mills also added to the study of free people of color through his article on issues related to research of them. Once again he used the Perkins, Sweats, and Goin(g)s as examples of a "nonwhite family of perceptible black roots."[15] Mills stated that darker-skinned people often sought out less densely populated areas, traveled in bands, and avoided places where they might be known. This observation confirms the reasoning for picking the Louisiana/Texas Neutral Zone.

A most helpful source of information comes from Paul Heinegg's extensive documentation of "Free African Americans" of North Carolina and Virginia. Heinegg has done an exhaustive study of free Africans and compiled listings of families and their genealogies where available. His work confirms much of the anthropological studies conducted by DeMarce and Mills. The Perkins family is identified in this volume through Esther Perkins who Heinegg suggests may have been born around 1712.[16] He also suggests that she died in 1748. However, at the time that Joshua Perkins was bound out, he and his sister are listed as orphans in the colonial records. I believe that many of the other children listed in the later records are grandchildren or nieces and nephews of Esther.

However, Heinegg's massive volume is excellent in laying out the laws of the times and amassing the names of free blacks. Among the records he accumulates are the names of Sweat, Ivey, Bunch, Goins, and Perkins, those

[13]DeMarce, "Very Slitly Mixt," 9.
[14]DeMarce, "Very Slitly Mixt," 18.
[15]Mills, "Tracing Free People of Color," 266.
[16]Heinegg, *Free African Americans*, 544.

familiar names of people who traveled to Louisiana in the early 1800s. He also outlines some important facts about racism in the pre-Civil War history.

(1) A number of white servant women appear to have had common-law marriages with African slaves. Among the names Heinegg identifies in this category is the name Perkins.[17]

(2) If you could pay taxes and were willing to go into the frontier, the color of skin was not important.[18]

(3) Restrictive laws on rights did not occur in North Carolina until 1826.[19] By then many of the Perkins had left for Louisiana. However, the "Free Negro Code" might have affected those who stayed behind.

(4) Free African Americans attended school with whites until 1835.[20]

This information suggests that the nation went through a cycle of racism, tolerance, and then racism, especially for mixed-race people. That cycle would not stop for specific families until their color had faded.

Of particular interest is the history of early cattle ranching in the Americas, the chief economic activity of the Perkins males from 1810 to 1900. While cautioning researchers not to overemphasize the contribution of West Africans to the style of cattle raising that existed in the North American continent, Terry Jordan makes a compelling case for the Fulani influence.[21] The Fulani or Fula(h) were originally concentrated in the West African region of Senegambia, with cattle raising as their primary occupation. When they began to disperse from the region, it was not a mass migration. Instead, they broke up into small clans. Jordan believes that if it is true West Africans helped shape the cattle ranching of America, it was through Fulani cattle raisers captured as slaves.[22] It is important to note here that the cattle-raising Fulani are described as tall, thin, and fairer in skin color then their African neighbors.

Jordan describes the Carolinas as the birthplace in the Americas of cattle ranching.[23] In the Carolinas was born the "cowboy" as well. According to this noted historian, the typical cowboy was of triracial origin. Jordan points

---

[17]Heinegg, *Free African Americans*, 4.

[18]Heinegg, *Free African Americans*, 5.

[19]Heinegg, *Free African Americans*, 15.

[20]Heinegg, *Free African Americans*, 24.

[21]Jordan, *North American Cattle-Ranching Frontiers*, 58.

[22]Jordan, *North American Cattle-Ranching Frontiers*, 58-59.

[23]Jordan, *North American Cattle-Ranching Frontiers*, 116-27.

to a "legacy that lives on in such lowland Carolina triracial groups or 'little races' as the 'Brass Ankles,' 'Red Legs,' 'Red Bones,' and 'Marlboro Blues,' 'Lumbees' (Croatans), and 'Buckheads' that belied the WASP image of the American cowboy." He also directly mentions the "red bone landowners of mixed white, black, and Indian ancestry in the settling of Jefferson County, Texas" and the Texas coastal plains.[24] The Red Bone landowners were the Perkins and their brothers-in-law, the Ashworths.

Based on this research, I felt satisfied that my ancestors came from the Red Bones of South Carolina, given their names, their migration, and their occupation. The Perkins name appears in the research lists for triracials and in the history of cattle ranching. They followed the migration path outlined in Terry Jordan's history of cattle ranching. However, how did the Joshua Perkins I had found in Virginia connect with the Carolinas? If I accepted him as a great-grandfather, it would account for the early designation of color in the family. What about the insistence on being Portuguese? Had the family just taken on the tradition of Melungeon people? Intermarriage with the Goen or Goins family would not take place for two more generations, as far as records show.

In January 1999, I received an issue of the Gowen Research Foundation's newsletter. The lead story was entitled "Research Find Offers Portuguese Angolans as Melungeon Link." The story tells of a California historian who has investigated early records from Portuguese sailing ships. The researcher, Engel Sluiter, discovered that the first shipment of slaves into Virginia were Portuguese Angolans.[25] The ship logs show that two dozen black Africans landed at Jamestown, Virginia in 1719. Although Jamestown is a considerable distance from Accomack County, Virginia, there were no large plantations in the Jamestown area and the slaves could have been dispersed inland. The ship was named Sao Joao Bautisto, or Saint John the Baptist. Was this the first Baptist in my family? A strange thought, but everything becomes so symbolic in exploring this history.

I believe there is a Portuguese connection in the history of the Melungeons *and* the Red Bones. The possibility of early Angolan slaves arriving could fit with an illegitimate mulatto boy born in 1732. It is also possible

---

[24]Jordan, *North American Cattle-Ranching Frontiers,* 189.

[25]Engel Sluiter, "Research Find Offers Portuguese Angolans as Melungeon Link," *Gowen Research Foundation Newsletter* 10/5 (Lubbock TX: Gowen Research Foundation, 1999) 1.

that Fulani cattlemen brought into the Carolinas are the source of the African blood in the Perkins line. Unless DNA testing becomes more sophisticated and widely available, the question will have no sure answer. But in my bones I know that part of my origins is in Africa. She sings to me, but that is another story.

Without commenting on Melungeons or any of the other groups, there appears to be constant intermarriage between mixed-race people in the Red Bones families, at least until the late 1800s. Some of them carried American Indian blood. They may have been Nansemond. There probably were Cherokee ancestors because that is the oral tradition in the family.

The story of Choctaw heritage is persistent among the Goins family members. My great-great-great-grandmother Jane Goen Perkins's brother tried to prove many years ago that the family descended from Philip Goins and a Choctaw Indian woman, Oti Montro.[26] Jeremiah Goins and his family wanted to be registered in the Choctaw Nation. At the time of the application, Jeremiah was said to be one-half to seven-eighths Choctaw. The Dawes Commission denied the family's request on December 1, 1896 because the family had not been residents of the Choctaw Nation and the descendants were not on tribal rolls.[27] The family appealed to the U.S. Court for the Southern District and won.

As for the white part of the line, it was probably originally English, given the place and time where they lived. However, "Old Jock's" wife was said to be Scottish. The intermarriage among the families was consistent with the early settlers of the colonies and the migration patterns thereafter, so that triracial people married other triracials for generations.

What did this odd mixture of people contribute to current family members? The answers can only be hinted at by looking at their relationship to the body of the land and the spirit of their being.

---

[26] *The Gowen Manuscript* (Lubbock TX: Gowen Research Foundation, 1998) 4203.

[27] *The Gowen Manuscript*, 4211.

There is a love of the sea
Deep within our blood.
The mystic call of the ocean
Which connects the flood
Of people traveling land to land
In search of some sweet place
That guarantees respect and freedom
For each and every face.

But do not be deceived.
The sea is not our core.
We are a landed people
Who stand upon the shore.
The sea, the mystic vehicle
Is vital to our quest.
It brought us to this land
And led us to the west.

And in the greatest moments
Standing in the wind,
The sea gives land a kiss
And toward her we do bend.
The land is oh so sturdy,
Providing food and care.
For Earth, the soul's mother
Embodies all we dare.

The smell of Earth is filling
The air with mother's scent.
Our ancestors shared that feeling
And through our blood it went.
Within us is a stirring
To capture what they knew
That sea and land and wind
Will bring us back anew.

Chapter 9

Sea, Land, and Wind: The Journey

I had been researching my grandfather's ancestry off and on for more than thirty years. Much of the time I would get off track and be involved in work, raising children, and participating in an all-absorbing life. Granddaddy was always with me, but his story seemed to wait for me to give it more attention.

For the next few years, I began to put the pieces together on an incredible story of migration, ethnicity, and bravery. As I built up files and bookshelves, it only made sense to go out and look at what I might find personally. So the odyssey that ended 1997 and began 1998 was born.

The other driving force for this journey was a need to see the land where my people had chosen to live. I had discovered a fascinating characteristic among the immediate family. We are in love with the natural world. Doing my master's thesis on how people describe their experience with nature had opened up answers to a question I had never asked. By including my siblings and my mother in the project, I had data on how they experienced nature. What I received from them was stunning.

All the participants in the study described a need to separate themselves from their everyday routine and physically move into a natural setting. Almost all of the study members felt some kind of intense connection with other species. More than half described a feeling of awe and characterized their connections as a spiritual experience. There was also language that emphasized a heightened awareness of the senses. Eighty-three per cent of my family members experienced the connection with other species and the heightened senses. What especially intrigued me was that more than seventy-eight percent of the group described a phenomenon I called "loss of identity" or "merging." I have since come to use the term, "dissolution of ego." Within the family members who participated in the study, all of them experienced a "dissolution of ego."[1] I am convinced that we have a mystical connection with the land and with nature.

A few years ago I attended my parents' church with my granddaughter, Anise. Mother was responsible for the "Children's Church," which takes place immediately prior the regular worship service of this Baptist church in Wimberley, Texas. She was describing Noah's ark and the beauty of the animals. She went on to show the children wildflowers that Anise had gathered for her. Mother talked about the ability to see God in each bit of nature, in the flowers and in the faces of each child sitting before her. I found myself in tears. My mother had just described the principle of panentheism, which is so central to Creation Spirituality. Seeing God in everything is not a Southern Baptist creed, and my mother never read the Creation Spirituality mystics who articulate this very principle. However, deep within her soul, she knew.

Thus the journey to see the landscape was shaped. Ken Strom, my husband, is a wildlife biologist and shares a love for nature. As important to tracing the migration route, were the stops, planned and unplanned, along the way to look at the landscape. Ken is the most meticulous of researchers when it comes to deeds and tax records, but we both wanted to "feel" the places to better understand what the Perkins and their families loved about the places they chose to live. Could we understand what drew them to certain landscapes? Our journey took us from Virginia to North Carolina, down to South Carolina and back up to North Carolina, across Tennessee, down the Natchez Trace of Mississippi, into Louisiana, and through Texas to Goliad. However, I have taken this story a little farther back because it seems to give some context to who these people might have been.

As noted in the previous chapter, the Cattle Fulani of West Africa disbursed from the Senegambia region by breaking up into individual clans.[2] The Fulani are primarily cattlemen, not farmers. Much of their trade is based on getting adequate crops from local farmers while they move over the landscape (photo 20). The cattle are respected in an almost religious fashion. It is their wealth and the legacy for their descendants.

I am not personally familiar with the West African landscape because, with the exception of Nigeria, most of my work has been in East Africa.

---

[1] Patricia A. Waak, "A Phenomenological Study of the Experience of Nature" (master's thesis, Regis University, 1998) 27.

[2] Jordan, *North American Cattle Ranching,* 58.

The tribe that I have observed which seems similar is that of the Masai. Cattle are their wealth also. The current rise in ecotourism in Kenya has made the local Masai even wealthier.

The Fulani and the Masai tend to be nomadic. By the time cattle started appearing in great numbers in South Carolina, the cowpen was instituted. The idea of penning up the cows was an African/British tradition that seemed to originate in Jamaica. The cattle could feed in the savannas of the Carolinas and in the tidal flats on the coastline in the winter.[3] The Perkins family lived around the swamplands. The nucleus of the cowpen culture from 1675 to 1715 had come up from the coastline and encompassed much of the Pee Dee River.[4] While Old Jock Perkins was not born then, he and his sons appeared in the Carolinas by the mid- to late-1700s.

The swamps of the Carolinas were probably not highly valued by landowners, so they are places that were available to free people of color. Both Old Jock and one of the Sweat's (another triracial family) bought land in this area. Land does not discriminate and does not see the color of a person's skin. Evidence shows that they were largely accepted by their neighbors as respected, law-abiding citizens. There is a clear history of buying and paying taxes on land and cattle. The earliest land purchase by Old Jock was on Wilkerson Swamp in Bladen County, North Carolina. Ken and I went to see the swamp, which today has interstate 40 running through its middle. It was lush and green even in early January, which would have made it a wonderful place to keep livestock and raise subsistent crops. The trees were oak and hickory, although pine trees were not far away.

I can only imagine the warm, summer winds that came up from the coastline. The deep abiding love for the sea must have been in the family's heritage, but they clearly were land-based people. The swamps and rivers provided water for the family and for the cattle and other livestock. Did they want more space? Or was the need for space met by traveling with the cattle at grazing time? There is a longing for spending days out of doors and traveling on the landscape. In our family there is also a great love for horses and cows.

Going through South Carolina, Ken and I went to Elizabethtown, North Carolina, which is in Burke County next to Robeson County, the home of the triracial Lumbee Indians. Here in the county courthouse, we

---

[3]Jordan, *North American Cattle Ranching*, 110.
[4]Jordan, *North American Cattle Ranching*, 111.

found evidence of Perkins and Willis as residents. Joshua Perkins sold land he had received through a land grant. It is not clear whether this was a land purchase or a grant made to him for Revolutionary War service. During the *Perkins vs. Smith* lawsuit, testimony was given that Joshua had fought in the Revolutionary War. History notes that General Francis Marion gathered together an assorted group of men and boys who were black and white from along the Pee Dee River to fight with him.[5] Many of these men came from the families that migrated to Louisiana years later.

We picked up a number of deeds and other records. We obtained the records of sales of lands that Joseph Willis transacted after he received his freedom. It was here that we obtained a copy of the emancipation bill passed by the North Carolina General Assembly.

On December 30, 1997, we arrived in Aiken, South Carolina. Aiken County is said to be the birthplace of several of Joshua Perkins's children. This Joshua Perkins was Old Jock's son. By then Joshua presumably had fought in the Revolutionary War and married Mary Mixon. Prior to that we only know that he was involved with Gilbert Sweat in Gilbert's taking away Frances Smith, John Barney Taylor's wife.

There were few records of those dates at the Aiken County Courthouse. The quaint library yielded up a number of books, including a listing of the Revolutionary troops of North Carolina. This place gave you a sense of the post-Civil War South. The streets were wide and long. Antebellum homes lined each side of the street and the town had planted different varieties of Southern trees along the boulevard. Sweet gum, oak, hickory and pine were among the trees. The Georgia State line is close by. Is this where the myth of the Indian woman born in Georgia began? Or is that in the Willis family line?

We did not stay too long but rather traveled north to Edgefield County, South Carolina. Some of my cousins' records suggest that my great-great-grandfather, Jordan Perkins, was born here. I staked out the historical society and Ken headed for the courthouse. There was little information available that we had not seen before. We were astounded that a small town had as big a genealogical base as it did. However, we did read from references that talked about Perkins's Ferry. Those references substantiated some of the other evidence we had read.

---

[5]Benson J. Lossing, *The Pictorial Field-Book of the Revolution*, vol. 2 (Rutland VT: Charles E. Tuttle Co., 1972) 479.

On December 31, 1997, New Year's Eve found us in Asheville, North Carolina at the base of the Great Smokey Mountains. It was snowing and beautiful. On New Year's morning we headed for the park. The first stop was in Cherokee, North Carolina among the Eastern Band of the Cherokee Nation. The reservation was covered with snow. Few shops were open, and most shops seemed to be geared for the tourists. There is a souvenir quality about them and they seem to be owned by white folks.

An exception is the Native American store run by John Wolf. Although there are the classic souvenir-type objects from other tribes, a lot of the merchandise is made by the East Band of the Cherokee Indians. In the 1800 U.S. census, Joshua Perkins was living with his family in Buncombe County, North Carolina. This county is part of the Cherokee reservation. How did they weather the snows? Our family has never been snow dwellers. Was their sojourn short in this area? Did the story of the Cherokee woman come out of their stay in Buncombe County?

Our intention was to cross the Great Smokey Mountains into Tennessee. Those plans got abruptly changed. It had been snowing in the mountains. One of the rangers said the pass had eighteen inches and Le Comte, one of the peaks, had thirty inches. We wandered around the visitor center and then went back into Cherokee to take another route to Tennessee. It reminded us that if Joshua and his family had crossed the Great Smokeys into Tennessee, they must have done it in the summer. Even then, it was hard to imagine travelling through the pass with wagons, horses, and cattle.

Newport, Tennessee seemed the place to spend the night on this January 1, 1998. We left early the next morning for Jonesboro with the notion that we might easily find the marker for one Nathan Gann, a many-great-grandfather on my grandmother Smith's side of the family. Gann is also a Melungeon and triracial-isolate name. We traveled south from Jonesboro, following the map to the Nolichucky River. The descriptions of a Gann Revolutionary War marker seemed to point to a farm and church near the river. We did not find any signs for the New Salem Baptist Church that was supposed to serve as a marker.

Traveling up and down the road, we finally decided to stop at a gas station and convenience store. The folks inside were friendly. However, there was no consensus over where the New Salem Baptist Church was located. After much discussion, one of the men called a friend who gave rough directions. The mother of this man does genealogy and took such an interest that she even looked up the Gann name in a local directory. A Ruth Gann still lives in Jonesboro. Meanwhile, one of her sons told us a story about Sam Houston. The man, his mother, and brother are related through a woman who was married to Houston. According to this gentleman, Sam Houston's wife was "high yellow," a term used for mixed race. My historical memory says he was married to a Cherokee at one point. Is that the same woman? How strange that there are so many stories of mixed-race people showing up? Is the interest in genealogy uncovering more history? Are we finally being honest about who we are?

We traveled down the road to our cutoff and saw a sign pointing to New Salem Baptist Church. We found the church at the top of the hill. A cemetery spreads behind the hill. According to the Gann newsletter, the Gann family gave the land for the church. I presume that means they were Baptist. However, nowhere around could we find the marker described in an old letter to my mother or in the notes I had taken. We traveled around the side roads for several miles and still could not see a fenced-in enclosure with the marker. The pastor was not at home. At this point, I called my mother. She had the Gann newsletter, and she read the portion from it. We were now sitting in the church parking lot again. Once more we walked around the cemetery, using binoculars to scour the countryside.

Ken decided that we should retrace our road tour around the church from the other direction in case we missed something. As we came back up the road north of the church, we spotted a man standing in his driveway. We pulled in and asked if he knew anything about the marker. He did. According to this gentleman, the marker had originally stood in the front yard of this very house. The man who owned the house was tired of it so he picked it up with his tractor and moved it to the side of the road by a tree. The story goes that when the tractor driver proceeded to move the marker, lightening struck. A number of years ago, a woman came from the historical society asked permission to move the marker up to the edge of the cemetery at the top of the hill.

Back up the hill we went. As we pulled into a gravel drive just below the cemetery, we found the marker. Nathan Gann served in the Revolutionary War. He is buried with his wife and daughter somewhere in a field below. All of the land we could see once belonged to him. The rolling hills spread across the horizon still untouched by urban sprawl and commercial development. It probably looks similar to the way it did when Nathan Gann farmed it. We stood for what seemed like hours soaking in the vista, embraced by the last patches of snow. No wonder I love the open spaces so much. It is in my blood.

After taking pictures and video, we reluctantly headed east to Carter County, Tennessee. Carter County's seat is Elizabethton. The most interesting piece of information was in a book on the history of Carter County. These books are all over the United States and are rich in information. Here I found the core of the controversies over Joshua Perkins. One family line claims a Joshua, or "Old Jock," as their patriarch; another says, no, he is theirs. The Perkins in Carter County show a line of descent that is disputed by one of my cousins. She believes that "Old Jock's" son was our Joshua. Others believe that "Old Jock" had a son named Joshua who was different from the Joshua who went West to Louisiana. My tendency is to side with my cousin since *Perkins vs. White* points to the names of Old Jock's children.

Clearly, there was a lot of investigation still to be done. The papers are in the McClung Collection of the East Tennessee Historical Commission library in Knoxville. So we were off to Knoxville on a Friday with hope that Saturday, January 3, 1998 found the library open. We spent the night in Knoxville and indeed the library was open. However, the T. A. R. Nelson papers were in a vault, which could only be retrieved by the archivist. She was not in on Saturday. We were disappointed but spent time perusing those endless volumes of census indexes and getting some more copying done. We would have to wait for a few more years to read the Nelson papers.[6]

We found the census index for Buncombe County, North Carolina. Tennessee had once been part of North Carolina. As noted earlier, Buncombe County is the county for the Cherokee Indian Reservation. Ken found two Joshua Perkins there in 1800. One of them was listed as a "free man of color."[7]

From Knoxville, we headed toward Nashville. We looked for the best place to connect with the Natchez Trace. South of Nashville the entrance to the Trace promised a scenic highway through woods, across streams, and past ancient Native American mounds. All indications are that Joshua Perkins, according to his own testimony, traveled with Gilbert Sweat and a

---

[6]Heightened interest in this case has resulted in the library making one photocopy of the original notes. Sally Polhemus, one of the archivists, was very helpful in obtaining a copy for me.

[7]U.S. Bureau of the Census, Buncombe County North Carolina Household Census, 1800.

number of other family groups. Historians say that they followed Joseph Willis to Wilkinson County, Mississippi, where they lived for a while in Woodville. Joshua's deposition in Gilbert Sweat's lawsuit indicates that they lived on the Big Black River.

The highway follows the Trace as closely as possible. There are historical markers all along the route. In some spots you can leave the road and actually walk on parts of the old Trace. The Trace itself was the trail used by French trappers and Indians as they traveled towards the lower Mississippi. The trail has sunken down into the ground and was covered with leaves. There was a sense of mystery about this journey. I could imagine six or seven families traveling together. There would be children, one of them my great-great-great-grandfather, Jordan Perkins.

The season for travel might have been spring or fall when it was not so hot. However, there is no indication of timing in their travel. They must have tried to stay close to the water. We assume they did not travel by wagon because the roads were narrow. One sign said that the trail was traveled by foot or by horse. It said that the travelers could make twenty to thirty miles per day. We could not imagine a family with small children traveling that fast. As night fell, I tried to think about what it would be like to find a campsite, build a fire, and eat a meal. They must have been exhausted from the long day's journey. What stamina and daring they must have had to endure such a trip.

We stopped at Bear Mound to see one of the Indian ceremonial sites. Mississippi was home to Choctaws, among others. Jenny Goins, Jordan's wife and my great-great-great-grandmother was said to be part-Choctaw. However, this mound predates any modern American Indians. Its origins are ancient. Did my ancestors see these mounds? What was their reaction? In the dark we drove a part of the old Trace. The trees formed an arbor over us as we wound our way through the woods. It felt like going back into the deep past.

One of our stops was at the stand where Meriwether Lewis shot himself and was buried. A couple of years ago, I had given a talk up in Montana on America since Lewis and Clark. It was ironic to me that when Lewis and Clark were making their journey, my family was on the Natchez Trace. Lewis later came back down the Trace heading for Washington. He had grown confused and was reportedly pacing up and down in his cabin. A shot was heard and the stand owner found that Lewis had shot himself. Not far away an obelisk sits among some pioneer graves. It is the resting place of Meriwether Lewis.

Back on the Trace, there continued to be an eerie feeling of actually traveling the route of my ancestors and wondering how they must have felt as they moved down through the Mississippi woods. By evening, the rain was pouring, and we had arrived at Natchez, Mississippi. The next morning was clearer as we set off for Woodville.

Woodville did not have much to offer in terms of information. It is a quiet little Mississippi town close to the Louisiana border. We don't know how long the Perkins family stayed there. However, there are a number of Perkins descendants in this area to this day. After deciding how to get across the Mississippi River (down to Baton Rouge), we headed for Opelousas. Opelousas was the record center for many of the people for whom we were looking. We headed straight for the courthouse.

One of our favorite people was the Opelousas Courthouse archivist. His name was Keith. We were never given a last name although I discovered it later on a book that he had coauthored about Creoles in Louisiana. There were several documents we wanted. First, we were looking for a copy of the original court case involving Joshua Perkins and his daughters. We also wanted a copy of the original marriage certificate of Jordan Perkins and Jenny Goins. We got both the documents. Keith Fontenot had the original documents of the Sweat case in which Joshua Perkins was deposed. So we also had him make copies.

This courthouse is a rich archive. Marriage certificates for many Perkins members were in the courthouse records. Included in the list were marriages performed by Joseph Willis. Meanwhile, Keith Fontenot has become very interested in this family. He has met other researchers and has gone the extra step of reading genealogical articles about the family. I was amazed at how much he knew.

A clear connection to Bayou Chicot showed up on some of the marriage certificates. Gilbert Sweat lived at Bayou Chicot, and Joseph Willis had a church there. Next stop would have to be Bayou Chicot.

Bayou Chicot is a small town in the damp Louisiana woods. Calvary Baptist Church was easy enough to find. Mrs. Terrell directed us to her husband, the pastor. Dr. Terrell has been the pastor of the church for eleven years. He wrote a history of the church for its anniversary.[8] He also kindly gave us a copy and told us what he knew about Joseph Willis. There are old pictures of the original church. Today the parking lot sits on the church's

---

[8]Terrell, *The History of Calvary Baptist Church.*

foundation. Calvary Baptist Church is the oldest Baptist church west of the Mississippi River. Dr. Terrell had ancient church minutes in a box in his office. The Louisiana Baptist Association in Alexandria, Louisiana normally keeps them, but he had borrowed them. It was exciting to see the original browned papers with comments about church business.

After spending time talking with Dr. Terrell, we were directed to one of the local cemeteries. We were captivated by the humid, wet climate around Bayou Chicot. It was similar to the Wilkerson Swamp area, although further from the ocean. At the local cemetery we discovered old graves covered with mildew and moss. A man named Keller gave the land for Calvary Baptist Church, and his family remains are the predominant graves in the cemetery. Joseph Willis's third wife, Mary or Martha (?) Johnson is supposed to be buried in Bayou Chicot. We did not find her grave.

However, it was a different story when we headed to Occupy Baptist Church #1, another church founded by Joseph Willis. The only information we had was that the church was between Pitkin and Glenmora. At Pitkin, Louisiana, we asked for directions. Finding the Occupy Baptist Church cemetery was an exciting moment. Reverend Joseph Willis is buried there. In addition, almost every grave bore the name of someone who was related to those original families moving down the Trace. There were many Perkins family members there.

As night approached, we said goodbye to the cemetery and headed to the Texas border, stopping in Jasper, Texas for the night. The next day there was a thunderstorm and we ended up spending the night with my sister and her husband in Conroe. Their house is the one I grew up in so it seemed an appropriate stopover. The next day we were off to Jackson County and then back to Goliad.

Goliad is a very old town with ancient live oak trees dotting the prairies (photo 21). The coastal prairie is where the Perkins went in Louisiana. The grasslands were interspersed by rivers. So the Perkins would have loved grazing their cattle between the Sabine and Calcasieu Rivers. By 1860, the cattle livelihood was concentrated in the Coastal Bend of Texas, where large herds outnumbered humans forty to one.[9] It was here that Goliad sat at the end of one of the major cattle drives. It was here that the cowboy actually lived and worked. It was here that Jordan Perkins and his sons settled. It

---

[9] Jordan, *North American Cattle-Ranching Frontiers*, 217.

was here that Jordan and Jane Perkins would die, along with my great-great-grandfather.

Open prairie, live oak mottes, a stream down the center of the landscape describes the place where Jesse Perkins is buried on Sarco Creek outside of Goliad. The ocean is not far away, and the air is humid and breezy from the sea's wind. If you went by horseback, you could probably reach the shoreline in a few hours. Or instead, the creek would serve to quench the thirst of man, woman, or cow. I love the sense of freedom that plays across the prairie grasses as they are brushed by the wind. The old live oak shelters Jesse's gravestone. Did his love for the land ache in his heart like it does in mine? Did he look into the eyes of his horse and hold a conversation without words, as we do with our animals? Do we all long for the freedom he had? A brother dreams of tall grass prairie. Another looks for solace in the ancient practices of an earth-loving people. And I stand on the shore watching the waves and feeling the wind in my hair, while thanking my mothers for grounding me in my love of the land.

(See map.)

May I tell you what touches my heart?
It is the sound of the wooden flute's plaintive cry.
It is the beating of the village drum
From some distant hearth I can not find.
It is the music rising through the rafters
of some small church deep in the woods,
A remembrance of faith not lost
But found in a thousand different prayers.
Do not ask me to see God/Goddess in just one form.
I see them in every place I look—
A leaf, a cloud, a puppy's wagging tail.
We are wrong to put the Creator in a box
And demand that this structure hold the truth.
Instead I call upon the flute
And drum to join my voice in praise.
For together we sing the faiths of our fathers and mothers.

Chapter 10

The Roots of Our Spirit

As a theologian, I believe that spiritual and religious underpinnings form much of our fundamental values and belief systems. Even though we may practice certain rituals and faith-based rites, we also carry customs handed down through the centuries. By understanding the contributions of our spiritual heritage, we can identify patterns that strengthen our faith today.

The Perkins were a spiritual people, sometimes grounded in the religious ritual of their surroundings, and other times grounded in the roots of a far older and deeper connection. In this chapter I choose to honor what I have come to believe are the traditions of my fathers and mothers across time. While I do not know the oldest tradition in my family, I am choosing to start with what I believe to be our African roots.

As far back as I can remember, there has been a deep personal hunger for knowing and understanding Africa. For most of my life I could not understand the meaning of this longing, but my mother had the same feeling. Before my entrance into the Peace Corps, she told me that her dream had been to become a nurse and go to Africa. Whether this is an ancient memory that underlies what it means to be human or a specific ancestral call, it was present in her and in me. The day I first stepped off the plane onto African soil, an unbidden thought entered my mind—I am home.

While reading the material and sitting in a class on Afrocentric spirituality, the response of my soul was one of acknowledgment. Was I hearing the call of my ancestors? The hints in the legends are that the Perkins people have descendants who came from the Senegal-Gambia area. The Goins's descendants tell stories of Angola. As for so many Americans— whether now called black or white—racism, unacknowledged marriages, and years of migration cloud the past.

So the search comes from the soul and recognition of those ideas and stories which carry resonance within each individual being. Out of the multiple cosmologies that form our heritage, we try to identify some of our spiritual roots in African stories. There are clear indications of the African heritage in the honoring of nature, the identity with other living creatures, the soulful music that permeates each generation, and the longing for justice that impassions each descendant of this line.

From the time of the Egyptians, nature was portrayed predominantly in every aspect of the journey of the human being. The sun, moon, river, oceans, and earth were part of the creation story in every culture. However, in Egypt the concept of life after death was a prominent part of the cosmology. It was this hope of eternal and everlasting existence that became part of Western religion. The weighing of the heart to measure one's deeds equalized individual humans. Your status, class, and wealth were far less important than what you did with your life. For the downtrodden, poor, and nameless, everyone had a chance at eternal grace. Given the history of my ancestors, this hope must have been a major promise in return for all the hardship they would encounter in the course of their journey.

Of that journey there is little written. There are the records of women bearing "illegitimate" children. There are whispers of children bound into servitude. A family story tells of an unnamed woman, probably part-African and part-Indian, who "married a white man." Her son, born a slave, becomes a pioneer Baptist minister. Another descendant fights in court to prove that his ancestors were Portuguese, not Negro. I believe these people were the American descendants of Africans who told stories, sang, and practiced ritual. Granddaddy was a dreamspinner, astrologer, and healer. Did these gifts come from Africa? Or are they a part of any person grounded in mystical being?

Much of what we know of the base for African religion is through oral tradition.[1] Documentation does exist. However, it is the practicality of the religion that speaks to daily life. The wisdom of the Egyptians connected with the practical wisdom and knowledge of tribal people. The matriarchal and matrilineal aspects of African spirituality must have meshed well with the American Indian. The same principles of unity, elimination of chaos, elevation of peace, creation of harmony and balance exist within both. However, the society of the living and the dead is so much stronger in African spirituality, even though Native American peoples talk of tribute to the ancestors.

---

[1]Molefi Kete Asante, *The Afrocentric Idea* (Philadelphia: Temple University Press, 1998) 58.

The Ghanaian Akan concept that each child is born with a destiny is a familiar one in my family. Whether that is a Christian concept or one that has merged with African and Native American tradition, it is a strong idea that we are not predestined but do have a strong purpose in our lives. Did the idea of reincarnation come from the Egyptians? The evidence of language connections between Egypt and the Akan makes it a valid question.[2] The Akan belief that one has to come back to complete one's destiny carries a resonance of truth.

The idea that good is dependent on how well we master elimination of chaos carries profound weight. This principle combined with the meaning of sacrifice is worthy of a whole book. I am a strong believer in the concept of the "family soul," as well as the personal soul. The story of the family is carried, with all of its problems, by each generation until one person is able to resolve the conflict or story. From the Akan perspective, each person then is responsible for eliminating the chaos, or resolving the conflict. The resolution of the problem will require the sacrifice of each member who takes on the responsibility.

Perhaps the greatest faults of modern American society are that we have abandoned community, lost our ancestral stories, no longer know how to eliminate chaos in the tribal sense, and are unwilling to sacrifice ourselves. We decry lack of responsibility to society as a whole, but our training ground is in the family. If we do not hold dear our obligation to our ancestral and familial story, how can we cherish our obligation to the larger society in which we live?

So if our destiny is not a good one, the Akan believe we can choose reincarnation. Do we reincarnate back into the same family? Or is our destiny in another community of heritage? When my grandson died, we saw him as an angel who came to teach us. The Akan see him as a messenger that will come back. Maybe we should look for him among us rather than search for his little face in that of strangers.

Among the Yoruba of Nigeria, you are not considered a human until named. In Northeast Brazil you are often not named until the age of five. The reason is that infant mortality is so high before the age of five. Perhaps the other reason is that the high rate of infant mortality is best explained by the Yoruba idea that the child is a messenger. And the Brazilian pantheon

---

[2]Molefi Kete Asante and Abu S. Abarry, eds., *African Intellectual Heritage* (Philadelphia: Temple University Press, 1996) 276.

of Gods is patterned after the Yoruba because of the early introduction of West African slaves.

In the early 1500s Portuguese settled the coast of Brazil. They had found the land for raising sugarcane. However, the local indigenous Indians could not withstand the hardship of plantation work. The western coast of Africa was raided and slaves brought into the sugarcane-growing states. The result was a triracial mix of people who also represented a unique spirituality and culture. Even today, a local farmer will engage in the rites of a form of spirit worship imported from Africa (*macumba, candomblé,* or *xango/shango*) beginning from Friday evening until dawn on Sunday. Each person then attends Catholic mass or Protestant services. (In Brazil each *orisha/orixa*—god or goddess, or guardian spirit—has a counterpart among the saints.)

However the richness of the Nigerian Yoruba ethical teachings is not catalogued in Brazil. It is an oral tradition. The *Odù Ifá* (scriptures)[3] makes several points that are a subcurrent among the Brazilian spiritual practices that have become offshoots of the original. The same ethical framework exists: the dignity of the human; the well-being of family and community; the integrity of the environment; and the community of shared human interests.[4]

Notably, the dignity and power of women is present in the ethical teachings.

> And when he gave her power, he gave her the spirit power of the bird. It was then that he gave women the power and authority so that anything men wished to do, they could not dare to do it successfully without women.[5]

Few other religious teachings give women such a prominent place of honor. In Brazil it is the *Mae de Santo* who is chiefly charged with the religious ceremony. The later references speak of the belief that any childbearing woman can give birth to a priest or even a god.[6] It was this process which could bring heaven to earth.

Grounding in the Earth may be the significant contribution of Native American wisdom as well. Granddaddy was always said to be a Cherokee.

---

[3]Karenga describes the *Odù Ifá* as "the sacred texts of our Yoruba ancestors."

[4]Maulana Karenga, *Odù Ifá. The Ethical Teachings* (Los Angeles: University of Sankore Press, 1999) xi.

[5]Karenga, *Odù Ifá. The Ethical Teachings*, 73.

[6]Karenga, *Odù Ifá. The Ethical Teachings*, 219.

My research suggests that the family may carry the genes of at least three American Indian tribes. What are the spiritual principles that bind the present generation to the Native American cosmology? I can only look at the calling my siblings and I experience, for there were no strong religious practices I can point to. However, the same principles that Maulana Karenga points to (see above) were part of our upbringing. The dignity of individual human beings is an important aspect of our value system. Each person regardless of race, sex, gender, or economic class is to be treated with the utmost respect. Is that attitude African, Indian, or Christian? It is hard to say, except that it was probably a stated Christian principle. It was not always a practice. I regularly saw individuals discriminated against in my church, especially with regard to race and economic status. The African part of my heritage would remember their own struggle for acceptance. The American Indian part of my heritage accepted this principle as an absolute.

Both the African and Native American family units tend to be tribal in nature. As a result, the well-being of family and community is an important spiritual value. Until my generation, almost all of my mother's and father's families lived close to each other. They came together for important celebrations and provided for each other in times of need. My mother told me that her parents often moved back into rural communities from brief sojourns in the city. The move to the city would be for the purpose of income opportunities. However, my grandfather preferred being close to nature, and he felt his sons would be tempted to get into mischief in the city. All of his activities were aimed at providing for this family.

The love of the environment, the concern for its integrity and the connection to nature are values shared by both American Indians and Africans. It is clear from our memories of spending time with Granddaddy that he placed a great value on learning from nature. He loved to just sit out in the evening and listen to the sounds of birds and animals. I have always loved sitting in the grass in the evening. Perhaps that came from him. I watch the animals and birds that show up in my life. They each bring a special message about what is happening around me.

Several years ago I went on a vision quest in the Collegiate Mountains of Colorado. I was supposed to keep a dream journal for two weeks before the actual quest. For some reason I could not remember any of my dreams. Instead I kept a journal of all the animals which came into my life during the two-week period. Each day something different showed up, and each day I received a message. Does my uncanny relationship with animals come from the Native American tradition of honoring and listening to the animal and bird brothers and sisters? I only know that I get great peace and spiritual depth from interacting with these beings of Creation.

Granddaddy did not only bequeath his love of animals and other aspects of Creation. He also spent those long evenings looking at the vault of heaven. Granddaddy was interested in the position of the stars and their astrological meaning. Those books that filled his shelves were guides to understanding people and events. The constellations of North America are different from those of Africa. Native peoples in this country have long used the stars to tell them stories about creation, guide them in their values, frame their culture, provide for ritual, teach certain taboos, and give advice on everyday life.[7] According to my mother, Granddaddy used his star knowledge to understand the people around him. Many therapists today use astrology as a symbol system in working with clients. My siblings and I look to the heavens for the wonder of Creation that they present.

While astrology is not the primary guide of my life, dreams and their interpretation are vital to understanding my soul's process. Cherokee and Iroquois Indians used dream interpretation in their spiritual practice.[8] Dreams are an opening to the soul's journey. Carl Jung's work on dreams and archetypes is a valuable part of my training as a psychologist. However, long before Western psychology tapped into dream information, the native people in this country saw dreams in relation to their religious belief system. My grandfather's interest in dream interpretation was evident in the massive number of books he owned on the subject. I believe he was a dream spinner, one of the old ones who knew how to understand and use dreams as part of the spiritual journey. This dream emphasis encouraged me to do all of my training analysis in dream interpretation. It is an important part of my spiritual practice.

Finally, the American Indian heritage gives me a renewed and enriched sense of personal ritual. I will review our Christian heritage in the paragraphs to follow and will remark on the presence of ritual in Baptist churches. However, there has never been the depth of connection to Earth for me like that which comes from Native ritual. Those who come from other faiths use incense, but smudging with native grasses stimulates a primal

---

[7]Dorcas S. Miller, *Stars of the First People* (Boulder CO: Pruett Pub. Co., 1997) 2-5.

[8]Vine Deloria, Jr., *God Is Red: A Native View of Religion* (Golden CO: Fulcrum Publishing, 1994) 197.

connection for many people. Rituals at a medicine wheel on a full moon are profoundly transcendent. Sitting on Earth with my hands in the dirt is an erotic experience. Speaking with Brother Magpie or Sister Fox is the most enriching of dialogues. Sleeping under the stars is the most beautiful of moments. Praying to the six directions brings my being into the center of Creation. To me these are some of the spiritual gifts of my American Indian heritage.

What of the Christian heritage my ancestors have given me? How did we merge the ancient values while Christianizing Africans and Native Americans in the United States? The ancestors of Granddaddy's family were brought to Louisiana in the early 1800s by Rev. Joseph Willis, who himself was mixed race. Why did my ancestors become Baptists and not some other Protestant or even Catholic religious tradition?

After the Revolutionary War, there was a proliferation of Baptist churches in the Southern colonies.[9] Joseph Willis had been freed from bondage around 1787. According to family tradition, he sold the land he received with his freedom and traveled to South Carolina. By 1791, he was referred to in South Carolina Baptist history as a minister. Willis's leadership west, his decision to pursue life as a Baptist minister, and his connection with other triracial people, would have made the Perkins and other families naturally coalesce around the Baptist church.

There are other reasons for choosing the Baptist church. Jordan describes the attitude toward "cowpen" people as being decadent and unchurched.[10] He is not the only one to report their activities as outside the realm of their more gentrified neighbors. Webster Talma Crawford went further in his description of the triracial people who made up this group.

> It is clear then that the Red Bone[s] cannot be merely half-breeds; they are fractional breeds with a different denomination for every mother's son of them. But their common denominator may be set down as that nucleus formed from the exiles of Los Adaes, the remnants of the Pirate Crews which infested the Sabine Coast, the strays from the dwindling Indian Tribes and escaped Negro and Apache slaves. This combination of blood produced a hybrid element of humanity whose cunning, treachery, and

---

[9]Vincent Harding, *There Is a River: The Black Struggle for Freedom in America* (New York: Vintage Books, 1983) 44.

[10]Jordan, *North American Cattle Ranching*, 117.

downright malevolence have not been surpassed by any people in the history of the world.[11]

There are accounts of recklessness, thievery, and fighting among the Perkins clan over the years, including in the current generation. However, this description is not totally fair. The Baptist church with its doctrine of redemption might have just been what even the scoundrel members of the family needed.

The core beliefs of Baptists in the Southern United States consist first in a personal encounter between Jesus Christ and the individual. Baptism by immersion is a nonsacramental ritual symbolic of death and rebirth. At the heart of this belief is religious freedom.[12] If the Perkins and Willis families had been discriminated against throughout their history, any freedom from the judgments of others would have been valued. Each Baptist church was an autonomous body that added to that sense of freedom. According to one Louisiana Baptist historian, "the genius of Baptist worship lies in its scriptural basis, its spiritual warmth, its ethical and moral demands, and its adaptability to the needs of the people regardless of their class structure."[13] Outrageous behavior or not, the Red Bones could find structure and acceptance in the Baptist church of the 1700s, 1800s, and 1900s.

More fundamentally though, the Baptist church offered three very important ingredients. The first was a sense of community. From the beginning these large groups of triracial people lived, migrated, and resettled together. This phenomenon continued into the 1900s, where pockets of family members and associates were found settled in one particular area. Today, the community around Pitkin, Louisiana still contains a concentration of Red Bone descendants.

The second major factor has to do with music. Almost everyone on the maternal side of my family has some musical talent. There are pianists, flutists, drummers, violinists, and many singers. The main outlet for their musical abilities is in the Baptist churches to which they belong. The celebration of their spirituality takes place through their musical participation.

Finally, the promise of redemption is a strong feature in the Baptist belief system. For a people hounded by injustice there must be a warm

---

[11]Crawford, *The Cherry Winche Country*, 21.
[12]Greene, *House upon a Rock*, 17.
[13]Greene, *House upon a Rock*, 18.

resonance to a theology which says you are accepted and embraced no matter who you are.

Although the tradition of the Baptist church has remained in my family until now, there has always been a mix of magic, nature, and nontraditional spiritual practice. Today there is little evidence of anything but European (white) in the family except in my grandchildren whose fathers are both African American. Our joy together is the search for the stories of our ancestors, their hopes and dreams, their journeys, and their soul. Each piece becomes part of a larger mosaic that sees the gifts that come from all our people, shares the sorrow of their hardship, and feels the hope of healing that comes from fulfilling our purpose.

The Path of Transformation

Chapter 11 is fully within this path that transforms our lives because it claims justice on behalf of my ancestors and on behalf of my children, grandchildren, and nieces and nephews. Connecting the ancestral gifts to my generation and me has been a spiritual journey. But the legacy is only complete if I can relate these stories and their gifts to the next generation. My granddaughter represents an unusual recipient since her heritage from her father is also triracial. In effect, this young girl completes a cycle in a time when she represents a particular story of America's experiment as a "melting pot." She also helps my family reclaim our lost ancestral stories with joy, dignity, and grace.

This final chapter is about reconciliation. I did not know how profound that reconciliation would be when I started writing this last segment. I began with focusing on the larger landscape. We will only have justice for humans and other life on Earth, if we reconcile ourselves with the past. Today, the world promises to be much more homogeneous racially. We must take away the otherness that has kept us from achieving a healing community. Modern society has stressed isolation and rugged individualism. Fox says that these "are lies that betray the very manner in which the universe operates."[1] If we are to practice justice for humans and nature, we must reconcile ourselves back to the idea of a living interdependent community. Part of learning this way of living again, is to recover the traditions and culture of the ancestors.

Reconciliation can be more personal as well. We bring together all the experiences of our lives and form a mosaic of meaning. That process is what I find myself in as I reconstruct my life and that of my family. I know that I am in a time of transformation, and the reconciliation of the family

---

[1]Matthew Fox, *One River, Many Wells* (New York: Tacher/Putnam, 2000) 437.

community has become the most fundamental path that I will ever walk. It calls to me from the depth of my hope and sorrow.

Granddaddy was a Cherokee.

Crossing the boundaries of myth
I am struck by the story we hold.
It creates within us a path
Of boldness, solidarity, exoticness.
Somewhere in the streams of truth and fabrication
Exists a tapestry.
It tells us of our specialness,
Our longing, our yearning.

In Portuguese it is "saudades,"
A homesickness without knowing where home is.
It sits in the form of memory of an old man
In his rocking chair on the porch.
What is your story?
Who are you?
What are we?
We long for reconciliation, for oneness,
For unspeakable union.

Granddaddy was a Cherokee.
Or was he?
As the pages of old documents and words of stories
Separate into a three-dimensional picture,
The lives of individuals, vaguely glimpsed,
Pulse with each heartbeat.

The truth is inside those tiny cells
which spell out my life.
What do I know from my own wisdom?

They were powerful, and their power grows.
They loved the land and all its creatures.
They filled their lives with music.
They carried the wisdom of the past and present.
They were reckless and rebellious.
They believed that God/Goddess resided in everything.
They practiced magic.
They were involved in respelling the world.
They yearned for reconciliation.

Granddaddy was a Cherokee?
He was every man and woman.
Yes, No.
Every tribe, every race, every creature.
He was, and is, our gift of life.

Chapter 11

Granddaddy Was a Cherokee

The last conversation I had with my mother included a request from her that we sing a duet at her church. I was planning to visit my parents in late March, before traveling to Philadelphia for a faith-based workshop. We laughed together about whether the song would be traditional or contemporary. We had sung together when I was younger and once I had joined her in her church choir. I did not know during that conversation that our last song would be one of our dying—and living. On a late Thursday afternoon in February 2001, my mother was felled by a massive stroke as she walked into her bedroom.

My mother did not live to see the completion of this book, but we shared documents we discovered. We weighed the truth of each one and examined what we knew from family lore and legal records. Those interested in genealogy as historical reference will appreciate the need to research every piece of information. I have tried to use the best research techniques for finding and connecting the disparate parts of the Perkins's journey from Virginia to Texas.

However, with any research we are at the mercy of duplicate names, changing ethnicity, conflicting family stories, and, in our case, no family Bibles, correspondence, or diaries. Fire was a greater hazard than migration. A fire in the Goliad County Courthouse around 1870 destroyed hundreds of records. Great-aunt Lucretia Smith Holbrook reported that a fire in the family home consumed photographs and legal papers.

In the end we are left with a patchwork of court cases, cemetery markers, county logs, and tax rolls. It is better than nothing. Filling in the gaps is done through patchy family recollections. However, without the story of Columbus Perkins, I would not have found important census data and my cousin, Shirley Conrad. We would not have known that Martha Mary Perkins Quarrels Smith was the daughter of Jesse and Lucinda Perkins.

When Martha married Charles W. Smith, she was listed as Mrs. M. M. Quarrels. Through that information we were able to track the movements of Martha and Charles throughout Goliad. And it was the memory of Rev. Howard Bundick that provided Lucinda Perkins's maiden name of Willis.

Although anyone could research Red Bones, the family connection makes the understanding of their story more potent. One of the few novels about Red Bones gave a different explanation for their ancestral make up.[1] I am certain that although we can not prove the actual percentage of DNA from each source, the purest Red Bone families are a large percentage European, a smaller percentage Native American, and an even smaller percentage black African. So many of my Texas cousins today have one parent who is of German descent that specific Red Bone characteristics cannot be generalized.

If we are to reclaim and recover who we are and who we are capable of being, we must bring back together our history and the connections to each other. The old stories will remain. My Uncle Johnnie repeated the tale that Granddaddy's mother was a pure Indian. Both my uncles had tales to tell of Granddaddy's courage and stamina, working fields sometimes and on army supply units at other times. Mother's notes expand on how Grand-daddy did not like the city. He loved living in the country and would retreat to farming whenever he felt city life was damaging his sons' values.

We bring together our past, present, and future in who we are and the personal stories we tell. Although the Red Bone ancestors were hidden from the family, their features are present in the high cheekbones, sometimes dark skin, and occasional tight curly hair. The clearest indication of their presence is in the strength, courage, and sense of community we exhibit. They are a tribe, although the part we know best is the Smith part. They are a religious people, mostly Baptist today, but their spirituality is deeply connected to Earth. Today, Red Bones awareness has generally disappeared except among some of those with Red Bones names such as Perkins, Willis, Johnson, Sweat, Dyal/Dial, Ivey, Bunch, Ashworth, and Goen/Goins. Most do not know their bones are red except in the deepest marrow of their being. To have red bones is to have won freedom. To have red bones is to sing your joy. We can claim our gifts because a group of people lived and loved and dared to hope for a better world.

In many cultures the color red is a sign of completion—the circle has closed. In a way, that is particularly true for me. My granddaughter, Anise,

---

[1] Carlyle Tillery, *Red Bone Woman* (New York: Avon Publishing Co., Inc., 1950).

is the daughter of an African-American man, Dion Savoy, and my daughter, Rachel. In fact, the Savoys of Maryland are known as "Wesorts," another of the triracial designations identified in a report written in the mid-1940s.[2] The term may come from an old saying that "We sorts are different from you sorts." Anise can claim that she has this tradition on both sides of her family.

Her long, curly, black hair and dark eyes combine with a slightly cream-colored skin to make a stunning beauty. Anise calls herself "mixed" as a race, and the U.S. Census Bureau today is accommodating a growing number of Americans who share this designation. Perhaps race will become less important as the years go by. One can only hope that we will be valued as individuals for our uniqueness.

But even as we merge into a society that is homogenized, it is really our family stories that will remain special. My father's ancestors were farmers. They came to this country to live on the land and practice their trade. For more than 150 years they have done so, living lives that commanded the respect of their neighbors. My mother's ancestors were cattle-herders. They wandered the country, in their disparate parts, and came together more than 250 years ago. They lived on the edge of society until they had totally integrated into the fabric of the Western myth. They too have commanded respect. What we today have inherited is strength, courage, daring, and a respect for the land that serves us and that we serve in return.

The Red Bones have not disappeared. They are no longer an isolate. We are here caring for the same things we always cared for: Family and Earth.

---

[2]William Harlen Gilbert, Jr., "Race, Cultural Groups, Social Differentiation," *Social Forces* (May 1946): 438-47.

Appendix

Ascendancy Charts

1. Charles W. Smith and Martha Mary Perkins

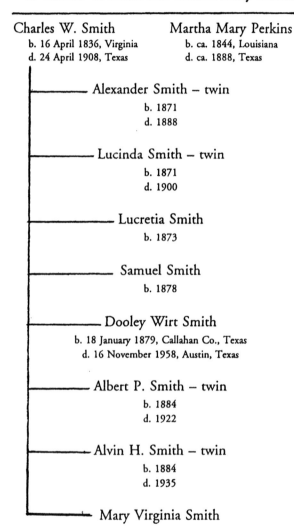

Charles W. Smith
b. 16 April 1836, Virginia
d. 24 April 1908, Texas

Martha Mary Perkins
b. ca. 1844, Louisiana
d. ca. 1888, Texas

Alexander Smith – twin
b. 1871
d. 1888

Lucinda Smith – twin
b. 1871
d. 1900

Lucretia Smith
b. 1873

Samuel Smith
b. 1878

Dooley Wirt Smith
b. 18 January 1879, Callahan Co., Texas
d. 16 November 1958, Austin, Texas

Albert P. Smith – twin
b. 1884
d. 1922

Alvin H. Smith – twin
b. 1884
d. 1935

Mary Virginia Smith

2. Dooley Wirt Smith and Annie Elizabeth Jane Mayes

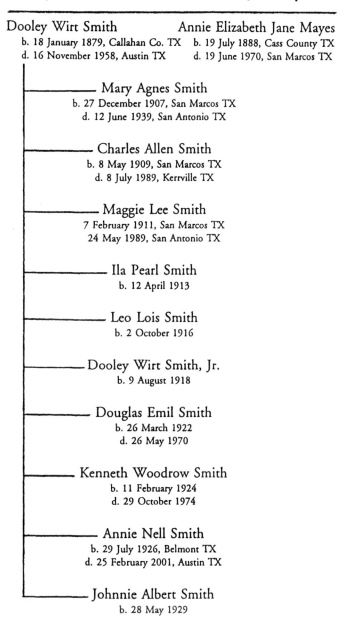

Dooley Wirt Smith   Annie Elizabeth Jane Mayes
b. 18 January 1879, Callahan Co. TX   b. 19 July 1888, Cass County TX
d. 16 November 1958, Austin TX   d. 19 June 1970, San Marcos TX

Mary Agnes Smith
b. 27 December 1907, San Marcos TX
d. 12 June 1939, San Antonio TX

Charles Allen Smith
b. 8 May 1909, San Marcos TX
d. 8 July 1989, Kerrville TX

Maggie Lee Smith
7 February 1911, San Marcos TX
24 May 1989, San Antonio TX

Ila Pearl Smith
b. 12 April 1913

Leo Lois Smith
b. 2 October 1916

Dooley Wirt Smith, Jr.
b. 9 August 1918

Douglas Emil Smith
b. 26 March 1922
d. 26 May 1970

Kenneth Woodrow Smith
b. 11 February 1924
d. 29 October 1974

Annie Nell Smith
b. 29 July 1926, Belmont TX
d. 25 February 2001, Austin TX

Johnnie Albert Smith
b. 28 May 1929

3. Boxly William Waak and Anne Nell Smith

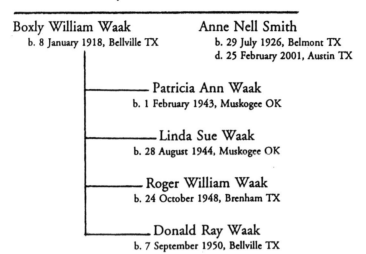

Boxly William Waak	Anne Nell Smith
b. 8 January 1918, Bellville TX	b. 29 July 1926, Belmont TX
	d. 25 February 2001, Austin TX

Patricia Ann Waak
b. 1 February 1943, Muskogee OK

Linda Sue Waak
b. 28 August 1944, Muskogee OK

Roger William Waak
b. 24 October 1948, Brenham TX

Donald Ray Waak
b. 7 September 1950, Bellville TX

4. Jordan Perkins and Virginia Jane "Jinny" Goen

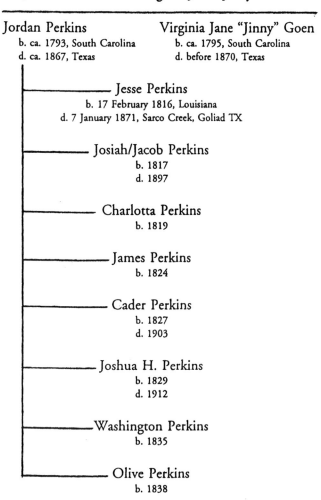

Jordan Perkins
b. ca. 1793, South Carolina
d. ca. 1867, Texas

Virginia Jane "Jinny" Goen
b. ca. 1795, South Carolina
d. before 1870, Texas

Jesse Perkins
b. 17 February 1816, Louisiana
d. 7 January 1871, Sarco Creek, Goliad TX

Josiah/Jacob Perkins
b. 1817
d. 1897

Charlotta Perkins
b. 1819

James Perkins
b. 1824

Cader Perkins
b. 1827
d. 1903

Joshua H. Perkins
b. 1829
d. 1912

Washington Perkins
b. 1835

Olive Perkins
b. 1838

5. Jesse Perkins and Lucinda Willis

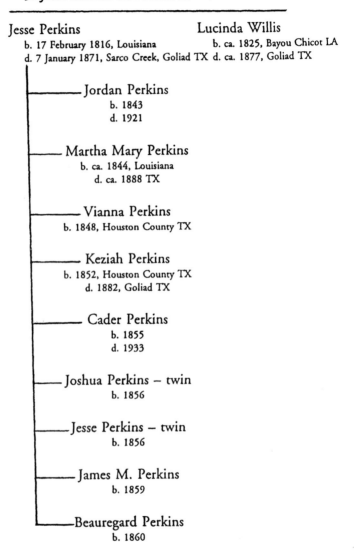

Jesse Perkins
  b. 17 February 1816, Louisiana
  d. 7 January 1871, Sarco Creek, Goliad TX

Lucinda Willis
  b. ca. 1825, Bayou Chicot LA
  d. ca. 1877, Goliad TX

Jordan Perkins
  b. 1843
  d. 1921

Martha Mary Perkins
  b. ca. 1844, Louisiana
  d. ca. 1888 TX

Vianna Perkins
  b. 1848, Houston County TX

Keziah Perkins
  b. 1852, Houston County TX
  d. 1882, Goliad TX

Cader Perkins
  b. 1855
  d. 1933

Joshua Perkins – twin
  b. 1856

Jesse Perkins – twin
  b. 1856

James M. Perkins
  b. 1859

Beauregard Perkins
  b. 1860

6. Joshua Perkins and Mary Mixon

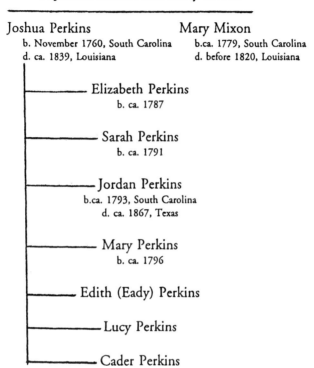

Joshua Perkins
b. November 1760, South Carolina
d. ca. 1839, Louisiana

Mary Mixon
b.ca. 1779, South Carolina
d. before 1820, Louisiana

Elizabeth Perkins
b. ca. 1787

Sarah Perkins
b. ca. 1791

Jordan Perkins
b.ca. 1793, South Carolina
d. ca. 1867, Texas

Mary Perkins
b. ca. 1796

Edith (Eady) Perkins

Lucy Perkins

Cader Perkins

7. Joshua "Old Jock" Perkins and Mary Black

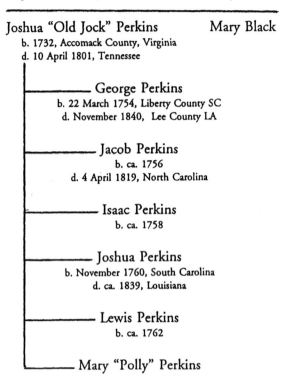

Joshua "Old Jock" Perkins   Mary Black
b. 1732, Accomack County, Virginia
d. 10 April 1801, Tennessee

George Perkins
b. 22 March 1754, Liberty County SC
d. November 1840, Lee County LA

Jacob Perkins
b. ca. 1756
d. 4 April 1819, North Carolina

Isaac Perkins
b. ca. 1758

Joshua Perkins
b. November 1760, South Carolina
d. ca. 1839, Louisiana

Lewis Perkins
b. ca. 1762

Mary "Polly" Perkins

8. Esther Perkins and Father Unknown

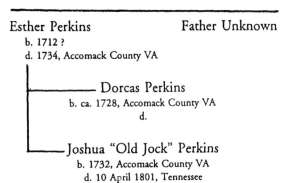

Esther Perkins   Father Unknown
   b. 1712 ?
   d. 1734, Accomack County VA

                Dorcas Perkins
                  b. ca. 1728, Accomack County VA
                            d.

              Joshua "Old Jock" Perkins
                  b. 1732, Accomack County VA
                  d. 10 April 1801, Tennessee

9. Patricia Ann Waak to Esther Perkins

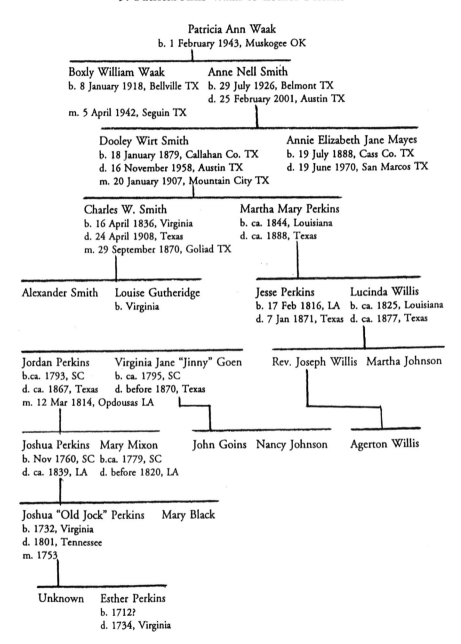

Patricia Ann Waak
b. 1 February 1943, Muskogee OK

Boxly William Waak   Anne Nell Smith
b. 8 January 1918, Bellville TX   b. 29 July 1926, Belmont TX
                             d. 25 February 2001, Austin TX

m. 5 April 1942, Seguin TX

Dooley Wirt Smith   Annie Elizabeth Jane Mayes
b. 18 January 1879, Callahan Co. TX   b. 19 July 1888, Cass Co. TX
d. 16 November 1958, Austin TX   d. 19 June 1970, San Marcos TX
m. 20 January 1907, Mountain City TX

Charles W. Smith   Martha Mary Perkins
b. 16 April 1836, Virginia   b. ca. 1844, Louisiana
d. 24 April 1908, Texas   d. ca. 1888, Texas
m. 29 September 1870, Goliad TX

Alexander Smith   Louise Gutheridge   Jesse Perkins   Lucinda Willis
                  b. Virginia   b. 17 Feb 1816, LA   b. ca. 1825, Louisiana
                                         d. 7 Jan 1871, Texas d. ca. 1877, Texas

Jordan Perkins   Virginia Jane "Jinny" Goen   Rev. Joseph Willis   Martha Johnson
b.ca. 1793, SC   b. ca. 1795, SC
d. ca. 1867, Texas   d. before 1870, Texas
m. 12 Mar 1814, Opdousas LA

Joshua Perkins   Mary Mixon   John Goins   Nancy Johnson   Agerton Willis
b. Nov 1760, SC b.ca. 1779, SC
d. ca. 1839, LA d. before 1820, LA

Joshua "Old Jock" Perkins   Mary Black
b. 1732, Virginia
d. 1801, Tennessee
m. 1753

Unknown   Esther Perkins
             b. 1712?
             d. 1734, Virginia

Bibliography

Accomack County Virginia Orders, 1744–1753.

Ardoin, Robert Bruce L., compiler. *Louisiana Census Records.* Volume 1. *Avoyelles and St. Landry Parishes 1810 & 1820.* Baltimore MD: Genealogical Publishing Co., 1970.

Ardoin, Robert Bruce L., compiler. *Louisiana Census Records.* Volume 2. *Iberville, Natchitoches Pointe Coupee, and Rapides Parishes 1810 & 1820.* Baltimore MD: Genealogical Publishing Co., 1972.

Asante, Molefi Kete. *The Afrocentric Idea.* Philadelphia: Temple University Press, 1998.

_____, and Abu S. Abarry, editors. *African Intellectual Heritage.* Philadelphia: Temple University Press, 1996.

Assessment of Property Situated in Bee County (Texas) for 1860.

Assessment of Property Situated in Bee County (Texas) for 1864.

Assessment of Property Situated in Bee County (Texas) for 1865.

Assessment of Property Situated in Bee County (Texas) for 1866.

Assessment of Property Situated in Bee County (Texas) for 1867.

Assessment of Property Situated in Bee County (Texas) for 1868.

Assessment of Property Situated in Bee County (Texas) for 1869.

Assessment Roll of the County of Goliad (Texas) for Ad Valorem Income and Salary Tax for 1869.

Assessment Roll of the County of Goliad (Texas) for Ad Valorem Income and Salary Tax for 1870.

Assessment Rolls of Property in Houston County, Texas Tax Records, 1846.

Assessment Rolls of Property in Houston County, Texas Tax Records, 1847.

Assessment Rolls of Property in Houston County, Texas Tax Records, 1848.

Assessment Rolls of Property in Houston County, Texas Tax Records, 1849.

Ball, Bonnie. *The Melungeons. Notes on the Origin of a Race.* Revised edition. Johnson City TN: Overmountain Press, 1992.

Bammert, Rosemarie, editor. *Cemetery Listings of Goliad County, Texas.* Goliad TX: Goliad County Historical Commission, 1988.

Benedict, David. *A General History of the Baptist Denomination in America, and Other Parts of the World.* Two volumes. Boston: Lincoln & Edmands, ?1813.

One-volume reprint: New York: L. Colby & Co., 1848. American Culture Series, reel 337.5: Ann Arbor MI: University Microfilms, n.d.

Bible, Jean Patterson. *Melungeons Yesterday and Today.* Signal Mountain TN: Mountain Press, 1975. Rogersville TN: East Tennessee Printing Co., 1975.

Birth Certificate 5643 for Columbus Perkins, 1947. Texas State Department of Health. Bureau of Vital Statistics.

Blair, Thomas. "Last Will and Testament." Accomack County VA. 12 September 1739.

Bladen Land Deeds 1210. Bladen County NC Courthouse, 1768.

Blockson, Charles L. *Black Genealogy.* Baltimore MD: Black Classic Press, 1991.

Bond hearing for "Chas. W. Smith" as County Surveyor in Goliad County. Commissioners Court, special session. Goliad County Texas Courthouse. March 28, 1889.

Boundary Survey. Goliad TX, Goliad County Courthouse. 1876.

Brasseaux, Carl A., Keith P. Fontenot, and Claude F. Oubre. *Creoles of Color in the Bayou Country.* Jackson: University of Mississippi Press, 1994.

Bundick, Charles. Personal communication, 1996.

Bundick, Rev. Howard. Personal communication, 1999.

Byrd, William L. *In Full Force and Virtue: North Carolina Emancipation Records 1713–1860.* Bowie MD: Heritage Books, 1999.

Certificate of Marriage: Sarah Perkins and Jesse Ashworth. Opelousas LA, St. Landry Parish Courthouse, 1810.

Certificate of Marriage: Jordan Perkins and Jinny Goen. Opelousas LA, St. Landry Parish Courthouse, 1814.

Certificate of Marriage: C. W. Smith and Mrs. M. M. Quarrels. Goliad TX, Goliad County Courthouse, 1870.

Certificate of Marriage: C. E. Bundick and K. Z. Perkins. Goliad TX, Goliad County Courthouse, 1871.

Certificate of Marriage: Chas. W. Smith and Mrs. Zilpha A. Holbrook. Goliad TX, Goliad County Courthouse, 1893.

Clark, Walter, collector and editor. "Daniel Willis Senr. to Gov. Caswell Respecting Admtn. &c." *The State Records of North Carolina.* Volume 11, 1776. Winston-Salem NC: M. I. & J. C. Stewart Printers, 1895.

Clark, Walter, collector and editor. "An Act to Emancipate Certain Persons Therein Mentioned." *The State Records of North Carolina: Laws 1797–1788.* Goldsboro NC: Nash Brothers, 1905.

Confederate Pension Application: Charles W. Smith. 2243. Texas State Archives, 1899.

Confederate Pension Application: J. J. Perkins. 27543. Texas State Archives.

Confederate Pension Application: W. B. Perkins. 2947. Texas State Archives.

Convict Record Ledgers (1849–1954), nos. 8389, 8390, 8391, 8392, 311, 2176. Texas State Archives.

Crawford, Webster Talma. *The Cherry Winche Country: Origins of the Redbones: and, the Westport Fight.* Edited by Don C. Marler and Jane Parker McManus. Woodville TX: Dogwood Press, 1993. Reprint: Hemphill TX: Dogwood Press, 2002.
(Crawford's work originated ca. 1932 and circulated as a typescript until it was edited and published in 1993. The original 1932 title was "Redbones in the Neutral Strip, or, No Man's Land, between the Calcasieu and Sabine Rivers in Louisiana and Texas Respectively, and the Westport Fight between Whites and Redbones for Possession of this Strip on Christmas Eve, 1882.")

Cresswell, Pamela R. "Perkins Trial" (transcription of selected portions of the Thomas A. R. Nelson Papers). <http://jctcuzins.com/pam/perkins/index.html> (1998, 1999, 2000). This home page includes Cresswell's introduction and links to the several parts of her transcription: "Trial Notes," "For the Plaintiff," "For the Defendant," "Instructions for the Jury," and "Verdict."

Death Certificate 13698 for Annie Mary Cowan, 1933. Texas State Department of Health. Bureau of Vital Statistics.

Death Certificate 0116 for Joshua Perkins, 1912. Texas State Department of Health. Bureau of Vital Statistics.

Death Certificate 0117 for Washington Perkins, 1916. Texas State Department of Health. Bureau of Vital Statistics.

Deed Records for Goliad County, Texas, V/495/497, 8 July, 1893.

Delaney Taylor versus Gilbert Swett. St. Landry Parish LA, District Court. No.1533, 1829.

Deloria, Vine, Jr., *God Is Red: A Native View of Religion.* The classic work updated. Golden CO: Fulcrum Publishing, 1994. Third edition and thirtieth anniversary edition, 2003. First edition, 1973.

DeMarce, Virginia Easley, " 'Verry Slitly Mixt': Triracial Isolate Families of the Upper South—A Genealogical Study." *National Genealogical Society Quarterly* 80 (March 1991): 5-35.

Doherty, Ila Pearl Smith. Personal communication. Buda TX, 1999.

Durham, Philip, and Everett L. Jones. *The Negro Cowboys.* Bison Book edition. Reprint: Lincoln: University of Nebraska Press, 1983. Original: New York: Dodd, Mead, 1965.

Duty, William. Personal correspondence, 2001.

Ericson, Carolyn Reeves. *Natchitoches Neighbors in the Neutral Strip: Land Claims between the Rio Hondo and the Sabine.* Nacogdoches TX: Ericson Books, 1985.

Fitts, Leroy. *A History of Black Baptists.* Nashville: Broadman Press, 1985.

Fox, Matthew. *One River, Many Wells: Wisdom Springing from Global Faiths.* New York: Jeremy P. Tarcher/Putnam, 2000. Dublin: Gateway, 2001.

_____. *Original Blessing: A Primer in Creation Spirituality Presented in Four Paths, Twenty-six Themes, and Two Questions.* Santa Fe NM: Bear & Co., 1983; reprint 1996. Reprint: New York: Jeremy P. Tarcher/Putnam, 2000.

Gilbert, William Harlen, Jr. "Race, Cultural Groups, Social Differentiation." *Social Forces* (May 1946): 438-47.

Gann, William R., and Gary R. Toms. *The Ignatious Nathan Gann Family: Three Generations of Pioneers. Including Families: Brumley, Layman/Lemon/Lemons, LaFollett/Follett, Massengill, Clark, Hicks, Harmon, Whisler, Green, Good, Winkle, Smith, and Delaney in Tennessee, Georgia, Alabama, Missouri, Arkansas, Oklahoma, and Texas.* Raytown MO: W. R. Gann and G. R. Toms, 1998. Third edition revised. Raytown MO: W. R. Gann and G. R. Toms, 2000.

Greene, Glen Lee. *House upon a Rock: About Southern Baptists in Louisiana.* Alexandria: Executive Board of the Louisiana Baptist Convention, 1973.

Guild, June Purcell; compiled by Karen Hughes White and Joan W. Peters. *Black Laws of Virginia. A Summary of the Legislative Acts of Virginia concerning Negroes from Earliest Times to the Present.* Reprint: Lovettsville VA: Willow Bend Books, 1996. Original: Whittet & Shepperson, 1936.

Harding, Vincent. *There Is a River: The Black Struggle for Freedom in America.* First Vintage Books edition. New York: Vintage Books, 1983. Original, 1981.

Hancock, Kaye. Personal communication, 1998.

Heinegg, Paul. *Free African Americans of North Carolina and Virginia, including the Family Histories of More than Eighty Percent of Those Counted as "All Other Free Persons" in the 1790 and 1800 Censuses.* Third edition. Baltimore: Clearfield Company, Inc, 1997. Other editions: *Free Afican Americans of North Carolina, including the History of More than Eighty Percent of Those Counted as "All Other Free Persons" in the 1790 and 1800 Censuses.* First edition. Adqaiq, Saudi Arabia: Paul Heinegg, 1991. *Free African Americans of North Carolina, Virginia, and South Carolina, from the Colonial Period to about 1820.* Two volumes. Fourth edition. Baltimore: Clearfield, 2001.

Hicks, William. *History of Louisiana Negro Baptists and Early American Beginnings, from 1804 to 1914.* Edited by Sue L. Eakin. Reprinted with new material added by the editor, with a biographical introduction by Bishop W. B. Purvis. Lafayette: Center for Louisiana Studies, University of Southwestern Louisiana, 1998. Original: Nashville: National Baptist Publishing Board, 1914.

Hillman, James. *The Soul's Code. In Search of Character and Calling.* Reprint: New York: Warner Books, 1997. Original: New York: Random House, 1996.

Houck, Peter W., and Mintcy D. Maxham. *Indian Island in Amherst County.* Second edition. Lynchburg VA: Warwick House Publishing. 1993. First edition, 1984.

Jordan (or Jordan-Bychkov), Terry G. *German Seed in Texas Soil.* Austin: University of Texas Press, 1994.

_____. *Immigration to Texas.* Boston: American Press, 1981; c1980.

_____. *North American Cattle-Ranching Frontiers: Origins, Diffusion, and Differentiation.* Histories of the American Frontier. Albuquerque: University of New Mexico Press, 1993; reprint, 2000.

_____. *Trails to Texas. Southern Roots of Western Cattle Ranching.* Lincoln: University of Nebraska Press, 1981.

Joshua Perkins Family Group Sheet. Curtis Jacobs Collection. Sam Houston Regional Library and Research Center, 2003.

Karenga, Maulana. *Odù Ifá. The Ethical Teachings, Translation and Commentary, a Kawaida Interpretation.* Los Angeles: University of Sankore Press, 1999.

Kennedy, N. Brent, with Robyn Vaughan Kennedy. *The Melungeons. The Resurrection of a Proud People. An Untold Story of Ethnic Cleansing in America.* Macon GA: Mercer University Press, 1994. Second revised and corrected edition, 1997.

Kapur, Sudarshan. *Raising Up a Prophet: The African-American Encounter with Gandhi.* Boston: Beacon Press, 1992.

Last Will & Testament of Thomas Blair. Accomack County, Virginia Courthouse, 1739.

List of Registered Voters of Goliad County of Texas, 1872.

Locklear, John. E-mail correspondence, December 2000.

Loridans, Sandra. Personal Correspondence, 1995–1998.

Lossing, Benson John. *The Pictorial Field-Book of the Revolution, or, Illustrations by Pen and Pencil, of the History, Biography, Scenery, Relics, and Traditions of the War for Independence, with 11 Hundered* [sic] *Engravings on Wood by Lossing and Barritt, Chiefly from Original Sketches by the Author; and with an Introduction by Terence Barrow.* Two volumes. Reprint of the 1859 edition; originally issued in semi-monthly parts, beginning in 1850. Rutland VT: Charles E. Tuttle Co, 1972.

McGowan, Kathleen. "Where Do We Really Come From?" *Discover* (May 2003): 58-63.

Marler, Don C. "The Louisiana Red Bones." Paper presented at the First Union, a meeting of Melungeons, at Clinch Valley College, Wise VA, July 1997. On-line at <http://dogwoodpress.myriad.net/dcm/redbone.html> or <http://www.multiracial.com/readers/marler.html>.

_____. *Redbones of Louisiana.* Hemphill TX: Dogwood Press, 2003.

_____. *The Neutral Zone: Back Door to the United States.* Woodville: Dogwood Press, 1995. Second edition, 1996.

Mbiti, John S. *African Religions and Philosophy.* Reprint with corrections. London: Heinemann Educational Publishers, 1989; original 1969. Second revised and enlarged edition. Portsmouth NH: Heinemann, 1999.

Miller, Dorcas S. *Stars of the First People. Native American Star Myths and Constellations.* Boulder CO: Pruett Publishing Co., 1997.

Mills, Gary B. *The Forgotten People. Cane River's Creoles of Color.* Baton Rouge: Louisiana State University Press, 1977.

_____. "Tracing Free People of Color in the Antebellum South: Methods, Sources, and Perspectives." *National Genealogical Society Quarterly* 78 (December 1990): 262-78.

Mullins, Marion Day, compiler. *Republic of Texas Poll Lists for 1846.* Baltimore MD: Genealogical Publishing Co., Inc, 1974; reprint 1998.

Nelson, T. A. R. Charge to the Court in *Jacob F. Perkins vs. John R. White* Papers in the McClung Collection. Knoxville TN: Knox County Public Library, 1857.

_____. Notes for *Jacob Perkins Vs. John R. White* Papers in the McClung Collection. Knoxville TN: Knox County Public Library, 1855.

Orr, Evelyn McKinley. "Evidence Links Red Bones and Baton Rouge to Melungeons." *Gowen Research Foundation Newsletter* 8/6 (Lubbock TX: Gowen Research Foundation, 1997).

Paxton, William Edward. *A History of the Baptists of Louisiana from the Earliest Times to the Present.* With a biographical introduction by Franklin Courtney. St. Louis: C. R. Barnes Publishing Co., 1888.

Perkins vs Perkins. Court of Probate. St. Landry Parish, Opelousas LA, 1837.

Perkins, Thomas. Unpublished personal family history. 1998.

Pitot, James. *Observations on the Colony of Louisiana from 1792 to 1802.* Historic New Orleans Collection. Baton Rouge LA: Louisiana State University Press, 1979.

Pruett, Jakie L., and Everett B. Cole, editors. *The History & Heritage of Goliad County.* Austin TX: Eakin Publications for the Goliad County Historical Commission, 1983.

Ravage, John W. Black Pioneers. *Images of the Black Experience on the North American Frontier.* Reprint: Salt Lake City: University of Utah Press, 1997; original 1997.

Rick, Brian. Personal communication, 2000.

Sekora, John. "Red, White, and Black: Indian Captivities, Colonial Printers, and the Early African-American Narrative." In *A Mixed Race: Ethnicity in Early America.* Edited by Frank Shuffelton. New York: Oxford University Press, 1993.

Shuffleton, Frank. "Introduction." In *A Mixed Race: Ethnicity in Early America.*

Sluiter, Engel. "Research Find Offers Portuguese Angolans as Melungeon Link." *Gowen Research Foundation Newsletter* 10/5 (Lubbock TX: Gowen Research Foundation, 1999).

Smith, Dooley W. Jr. Personal communication, 1998.

Smith, Johnnie. Personal communication, 1998.

Smith, T. Lynn, and Homer Lee Hitt. *The People of Louisiana.* Baton Rouge LA: Louisiana State University Press, 1952.

St. Amant, C. Penrose. *A Short History of Louisiana Baptists.* Nashville: Broadman Press, 1948.

State of Texas vs Henry Perkins et al. Goliad County Court 1244 (1878).

State of Texas vs Cato Perkins, James Perkins, Joshua Perkins, and Alex Linney. Goliad County Court 1280 (1879).

Stick, David. *Roanoke Island: The Beginnings of English America.* Chapel Hill NC: University of North Carolina Press, 1983.

Strother, Greene W. "About Joseph Willis." Master's thesis, School of Theology, the Baptist Bible Institute [later New Orleans Baptist Theological Seminary], 1934.

Teish, Luisah. *Jambalaya. The Natural Woman's Book of Personal Charms and Practical Rituals.* First edition. San Francisco: Harper & Row, 1985. First Harper Collins paperback. San Francisco: HarperSanFrancisco, 1988.

Terrell, Leon D. M. *The History of Calvary Baptist Church at Bayou Chicot.* Villa Platt LA: L. Terrell, 1992.

Tenzer, Lawrence Raymond. *A Completely New Look at Interracial Sexuality. Public Opinion and Select Commentaries.* Manahawkin NJ: Scholars Publishing House, 1990.

_____. *The Forgotten Cause of the Civil War: A New Look at the Slavery Issue.* Manahawkin NJ: Scholars Publishing House, 1997.

Thornton, Michael C. "Is Multiracial Status Unique? The Personal and Social Experience." In *Race, Class, and Gender: An Anthology.* Second edition. Edited by Margaret L. Andersen and Patricia Hill Collins. New York: Wadsworth Publishing Company, 1995. First edition, 1992. Fifth edition, 2004.

Tillery, Carlyle. *Red Bone Woman. A Novel.* Avon reprint edition. New York: Avon Publishing Co., Inc., 1951. Original: New York: J. Day, 1950.

Townsend, Leah. *South Carolina Baptists, 1670–1805.* Baltimore: Clearfield Publishing Co., 1935.

U.S. Bureau of the Census. Accomack Parish, Virginia Household Enumeration, 1800.

U.S. Bureau of the Census. Buncombe County, North Carolina Household Census, 1800.

U.S. Bureau of the Census. Free Inhabitants in Beeville in the County of Bee of Texas. July 9 and 10, 1860.

U.S. Bureau of the Census, Heads of Families—South Carolina. Cheraw District, 1790.

U.S. Bureau of the Census. Houston County, Texas Household Census. 1850.

U.S. Bureau of the Census. Inhabitants of Precinct 5 of the County of DeWitt of Texas. August, 1870.

U.S. Bureau of the Census. Inhabitants in Commissioners Precinct No. 2, Goliad County. June 22 and 23, 1880.

U.S. Bureau of the Census. Inhabitants in the County of Goliad County, Texas. August 6-8, 1870.

U.S. Bureau of the Census. Inhabitants in 3rd Precinct in the County of Callahan. Texas. June 23, 1880.

U.S. Bureau of the Census. Productions of Agriculture in Beeville Precinct in the County of Bee in the Post Office of Beeville. 1860.

U.S. Bureau of the Census, Rapides Parish, Louisiana Household Census. 1840.

U.S. Bureau of the Census. St. George's Parish. Virginia Household Enumeration, 1800.

U.S. Bureau of the Census. St Landry Parish, Louisiana Household Census. 1830.

U.S. Bureau of the Census. St. Landry Parish, Louisiana Household Census. 1820.

U.S. Bureau of the Census. St. Landry Parish, Louisiana Household Census. 1810.

Waak, Boxly. Personal communication, 1996–2001.

Waak, Nell Smith. Personal communication, 1996–2001.

Waak, Patricia A. "A Phenomenological Study of the Experience of Nature." Master's thesis, the School of Professional Studies, Regis University, 1998.

Waak, Roger. Personal communication, 1998.

Walton-Raji, Angela Y. *Black Indian Genealogy Research: African American Ancestors among the Five Civilized Tribes.* Bowie MD: Heritage Books, Inc., 1993.

Willis, Randy (Randall Lee). "Joseph Willis: First Baptist Preacher of the Word West of the Mississippi River." Wimberley TX: unpublished manuscript, 1998. Now published online as "Joseph Willis, the Apostle to the Opelousas, the First Baptist Preacher of the Gospel of Jesus Christ West of the Mississippi River," <http://www.randywillis.org/joseph.html> (c2000).

_____. E-mail correspondence, 2000.

_____. Personal communication, 1999–2000.

Wise, Erbon W. Personal communication, 1998.

_____. *Sweat Families of the South.* Sulphur LA: E. W. Wise, 1983. Revised edition, 1998. Reprint, 2002.

Work, Monroe Nathan, editor. *Negro Year Book. An Annual Encyclopedia of the Negro, 1921–1922.* Sixth edition. Tuskegee AL: Negro Year Book Publishing Co., 1922. Microfiche: (Series) Black Biographical Dictionaries, 1790–1950 no. 195. Alexandria VA: Chadwyck-Healey, 1987.

Yarber, Leo Lois Smith, Personal communication, 1998.

Index

Printed in the United States
222016BV00005B/92/A